Student's Solutions Manual to Accompany

Languages and Machines

An Introduction to the
Theory of Computer Science

Thomas A. Sudkamp
Alan Cotterman

Wright State University

ADDISON-WESLEY PUBLISHING COMPANY
Reading, Massachusetts • Menlo Park, California • New York
Don Mills, Ontario • Wokingham, England • Amsterdam • Bonn • Sydney
Singapore • Tokyo • Madrid • San Juan

Reprinted with corrections February, 1989
Copyright © 1988 by Addison-Wesley Publishing Company

ISBN 0-201-15769-1

3 4 5 6 7 8 9 10 AL 9594939291

Preface

This manual was written to accompany *Languages and Machines: An Introduction to the Theory of Computer Science.* Acquiring a thorough understanding of the topics that comprise the foundations of computer science is not a passive undertaking; active participation is required. This participation takes several forms; understanding the theorems and their proofs, following the techniques used to solve the problems posed in the examples in the text, and solving problems on your own. It is the ability to do the latter that exhibits proficiency with the material. This manual is designed to assist the reader in developing the ability to solve problems in formal language and computability theory.

Solutions are given for over 100 exercises. The problems in this manual were chosen to complement the examples presented in the text. The solutions are designed to illustrate general strategies for solving the particular type of problem. Understanding the techniques demonstrated in this manual should provide valuable insights that can be used in solving many of the other exercises.

Contents

Chapter 1

Mathematical Preliminaries

4. We prove that $\overline{X} \cap \overline{Y} = \overline{(X \cup Y)}$. This requires establishing both of the inclusions $\overline{X} \cap \overline{Y} \subseteq \overline{(X \cup Y)}$ and $\overline{(X \cup Y)} \subseteq \overline{X} \cap \overline{Y}$.

i) Let $a \in \overline{X} \cap \overline{Y}$. By the definition of intersection $a \in \overline{X}$ and $a \in \overline{Y}$. Thus $a \notin X$ and $a \notin Y$. It follows that $a \in \overline{(X \cup Y)}$.

ii) Assume $a \in \overline{(X \cup Y)}$. Then $a \notin X \cup Y$. This implies that $a \notin X$ and $a \notin Y$. Consequently, $a \in \overline{X} \cap \overline{Y}$.

A completely analogous argument can be used to establish the equality of the sets $\overline{(X \cap Y)}$ and $\overline{X} \cup \overline{Y}$.

6. The set of non-negative rational numbers is defined by

$$\{n/m \mid n \in \mathbf{N}, m \in \mathbf{N} - \{0\}\}$$

A rational number n/m can be represented by the ordered pair $[n, m]$. This representation defines a one-to-one correspondence between the rational numbers and the set $\mathbf{N} \times (\mathbf{N} - \{0\})$. The latter set is known to be countable by Theorem 1.3.3.

8. We first note that every real number in $(0, 1]$ can be expressed as a decimal $.x_0 x_1 x_2 \ldots x_n \ldots$. Note that the number $\frac{1}{2}$ is represented by both $.50000\ldots$ and $.49999\ldots$. To obtain a unique representation, we consider only decimal expansions that do not end with an infinite sequence of zeros. With this unique decimal representation, two numbers are distinct if they differ at any position in the decimal expansion. A

Assume the set of real numbers in $(0, 1]$ is countable. This implies that there is a sequence

$$r_0, r_1, r_2, \ldots, r_n, \ldots$$

that contains all of these values. Let $.x_{n0}x_{n1}x_{n2}\ldots$ be the decimal expansion of r_n. Construct the infinite two-dimensional array, the ith row of which consists of the expansion of r_i.

$$
\begin{array}{rcccc}
r_0 = & x_{00} & x_{01} & x_{02} & \ldots \\
r_1 = & x_{10} & x_{11} & x_{12} & \ldots \\
r_2 = & x_{20} & x_{21} & x_{22} & \ldots \\
\vdots & \vdots & \vdots & \vdots &
\end{array}
$$

A real number $r = x_0 x_1 \ldots$ is defined using the diagonal elements of the array.

$$x_i = \begin{cases} 0 & \text{if } x_{ii} \neq 0 \\ 1 & \text{if } x_{ii} = 0 \end{cases}$$

Clearly $r \neq r_i$ for any i since the ith position of r, x_i, is not identical to the ith position of r_i. Therefore the assumption fails, and we conclude that the set is uncountable.

11. Diagonalization is used to prove that there are an uncountable number of monotone increasing functions. Assume that the set of monotone increasing functions is countable. Then these functions can be listed in a sequence $f_0, f_1, f_2, \ldots, f_n, \ldots$. Define a function f as follows:

$$
\begin{aligned}
f(0) &= f_0(0) + 1 \\
f(i) &= f_i(i) + f(i-1)
\end{aligned}
$$

for $i > 0$. Since $f_i(i) > 0$, it follows that $f(i) > f(i-1)$ for all i.

Clearly $f(i) \neq f_i(i)$ for any i, contradicting the assumption that f_0, $f_1, \ldots, f_n, \ldots$, exhaustively enumerates the monotone increasing functions. Consequently, the set is uncountable.

14. The product of two natural numbers can be defined recursively using addition and the successor operator s.

basis: if $n = 0$ then $m \cdot n = 0$

recursive step: $m \cdot s(n) = m + (m \cdot n)$

closure: $m \cdot n = k$ only if this equality can be obtained from $m \cdot 0 = 0$ using finitely many applications of the recursive step.

17. Let L be the set of the points in $\mathbf{N} \times \mathbf{N}$ on the line defined by $n = 3 \cdot m$. L can be defined recursively by

basis: $[0, 0] \in L$.

recursive step: If $[m, n] \in L$, then $[s(m), s(s(s(n)))] \in L$.

closure: $[m, n] \in L$ only if it can be obtained from $[0, 0]$ using finitely many applications of the recursive step.

21. We prove, by induction on n, that

$$\sum_{i=0}^{n} 2^i = 2^{n+1} - 1$$

basis: The basis is $n = 0$.

$$\sum_{i=0}^{0} 2^i = 2^0 = 2^1 - 1 = 1$$

inductive hypothesis: Assume, for all values $k = 1, 2, \ldots, n$, that

$$\sum_{i=0}^{k} 2^i = 2^{k+1} - 1$$

inductive step: We need to show that

$$\sum_{i=0}^{n+1} 2^i = 2^{(n+1)+1} - 1$$

$$\begin{aligned}
\sum_{i=0}^{n+1} 2^i &= \sum_{i=0}^{n} 2^i + 2^{n+1} \\
&= 2^{n+1} - 1 + 2^{n+1} \qquad \text{'inductive hypothesis'} \\
&= 2 \cdot 2^{n+1} - 1 \\
&= 2^{(n+1)+1} - 1
\end{aligned}$$

24. The set R of nodes *reachable* from a given node x in a directed graph is defined recursively from the adjacency relation A.

basis: $x \in R$.

recursive step: If $y \in R$ and $[y, z] \in A$, then $z \in R$.

closure: $y \in R$ only if y can be obtained from x by finitely many applications of the recursive step.

27. a) The depth of the tree is 4.

b) The set of ancestors of x_{11} is $\{x_{11}, x_7, x_2, x_1\}$.

c) The minimal common ancestor of x_{14} and x_{11} is x_2; of x_{15} and x_{11} is x_1.

d) The subtree generated by x_2 consists of the arcs $\langle x_2, x_5 \rangle$, $\langle x_2, x_6 \rangle$, $\langle x_2, x_7 \rangle$, $\langle x_5, x_{10} \rangle$, $\langle x_7, x_{11} \rangle$, and $\langle x_{10}, x_{14} \rangle$.

e) The frontier is the set $\{x_{14}, x_6, x_{11}, x_3, x_8, x_{12}, x_{15}, x_{16}\}$.

29. Induction on the depth of the tree is used to prove that a *complete binary tree* T of depth n has $2^{n+1} - 1$ nodes. Let $nodes(T)$ and $leaves(T)$ denote the number of nodes and leaves in a tree T.

basis: The basis consists of trees of depth zero; that is, trees consisting solely of the root. For any such tree T, $nodes(T) = 1 = 2^1 - 1$.

inductive hypothesis: Assume that every complete binary tree T of depth n or less satisfies $nodes(T) = 2^{n+1} - 1$.

inductive step: Let T be a complete binary tree of depth $n + 1, n > 0$. We need to show that $nodes(T) = 2^{(n+1)+1} - 1$. T is obtained by adding two children to each leaf of a complete binary tree T′ of depth n. Since T′ is complete binary, it is also strictly binary and

$$leaves(T') = (nodes(T') + 1)/2$$

from Exercise 28. Thus

$$
\begin{aligned}
nodes(T) &= nodes(T') + 2 \cdot leaves(T') \\
&= nodes(T') + 2 \cdot [(nodes(T') + 1)/2] \quad \text{'Exercise 28'} \\
&= nodes(T') + nodes(T') + 1 \\
&= 2 \cdot nodes(T') + 1 \\
&= 2 \cdot 2^{n+1} - 1 \quad \text{'inductive hypothesis'} \\
&= 2^{(n+1)+1} - 1
\end{aligned}
$$

Chapter 2

Languages and Regular Expressions

1. Let X denote the set of strings over $\Sigma = \{a, b\}$ that have the same number of a's and b's. The set X can be defined recursively as follows:

basis: $\lambda \in X$

recursive step: Let $x \in X$. If $x = uvw$ where $u, v, w \in \Sigma^*$ then
i) $uavbw \in X$

ii) $ubvaw \in X$.

closure: A string x is in X only if it can be obtained from λ using a finite number of applications of the recursive step.

Cleary, every string generated by the preceding definition has the same number of a's and b's. A proof by induction on the length of the string demonstrates that every string in X is produced by the definition. Note that all strings in X have even length.

basis: The basis consists of string in X with length zero. The null string is the only such string and is generated by the recursive step of the definition.

inductive hypothesis: Assume that all strings in X of length k, $0 \le k \le n$, are produced by the definition.

inductive step: Let $x \in X$ be a string of length $n + 2$. Since x contains at least two elements and has the same number of a's and b's, x can be written $uavbw$ or $ubvaw$ for some $u, v, w \in \Sigma^*$. It follows that uvw is in X and, by the inductive hypothesis, is generated by the definition. One additional application of the recursive step produces x.

5

3. Let P denote the set of palindromes defined recursively in Exercise 3 and let $W = \{w \in \Sigma^* \mid w = w^R\}$. Establishing the set equality requires demonstrating that each of the sets is a subset of the other.

We begin by proving that $P \subseteq W$. The proof is by induction on the number of applications of the recursive step in the definition of palindrome required to generate the string.

basis: The basis consists of strings of P that are generated with no applications of the recursive step. This set consists of λ and a, for every $a \in \Sigma$. Clearly, $w = w^R$ for every such string.

inductive hypothesis: Assume that every string generated by n or fewer applications of the recursive step is in W.

inductive step: Let u be a string generated by $n+1$ applications of the recursive step. Then $u = awa$ for some string w generated by n applications. Thus,

$$
\begin{aligned}
w^R &= (awa)^R \\
&= a^R w^R a^R && \text{'Theorem 2.1.6'} \\
&= aw^R a \\
&= awa && \text{'inductive hypothesis'}
\end{aligned}
$$

We now show that $W \subseteq P$. The proof is by induction on the length of the strings in W.

basis: If $length(u) = 0$ then $w = \lambda$ and $\lambda \in P$ by the basis of the recursive definition. Similarly, strings of length one in W are also in P.

inductive hypothesis: Assume that every string $w \in W$ with length n or less is in P.

inductive step: Let $w \in W$ be a string of length $n + 1$. Then w can be written ua where $length(u) = n \geq 1$. Taking the reversal,

$$
w = w^R = (ua)^R = au^R
$$

Since w begins and ends with same symbol, it may be written $w = ava$. Again, using reversals we get

$$
\begin{aligned}
w^R &= (ava)^R \\
&= a^R v^R a^R \\
&= av^R a
\end{aligned}
$$

Since $w = w^R$, we conclude that $ava = av^R a$ and $v = v^R$. By the inductive hypothesis, $v \in P$. It follows, from the recursive step in the definition of P, that $w = ava$ is also in P.

5. We prove, by induction on the length of the string, that $w = (w^R)^R$ for every string $w \in \Sigma^*$.

basis: The basis consists of the null string. In this case, $(\lambda^R)^R = (\lambda)^R = \lambda$ as desired.

inductive hypothesis: Assume that $(w^R)^R = w$ for all strings $w \in \Sigma^*$ of length n or less.

inductive step: Let w be a string of length $n + 1$. Then $w = ua$ and

$$
\begin{aligned}
(w^R)^R &= ((ua)^R)^R \\
&= (a^R u^R)^R && \text{`Theorem 2.1.6'} \\
&= (au^R)^R \\
&= (u^R)^R a^R && \text{`Theorem 2.1.6'} \\
&= ua^R && \text{`inductive hypothesis'} \\
&= ua \\
&= w
\end{aligned}
$$

9. Every aa in the strings defined by the regular expression $(b \cup ab \cup aab)^*$ is followed by at least one b. Thus the expression

$$(b \cup ab \cup aab)^*(\lambda \cup a \cup aa)$$

represents the set of all strings over $\{a, b\}$ that do not contain the substring aaa.

11. The leading a and trailing cc are explicitly placed in the expression

$$a(a \cup c)^* b(a \cup c)^* b(a \cup c)^* cc$$

Any number of a's and c's, represented by the expression $(a \cup c)^*$, may surround the two b's.

14. The set of strings over $\{a, b\}$ that contain the substrings aa and bb is represented by

$$(a \cup b)^* aa(a \cup b)^* bb(a \cup b)^* \cup (a \cup b)^* bb(a \cup b)^* aa(a \cup b)^*$$

The two expressions joined by the $\cup$ indicate that the aa may precede or follow the bb.

21. The regular expression $(b^* ab^* a)^* b^* \cup (a^* ba^* b)^* a^* ba^*$ defines strings over $\{a, b\}$ with an even number of a's or an odd number of b's. This expression is obtained by combining an expression for each of the component subsets with the union operator.

25. To obtain an expression for the strings over $\{a, b, c\}$ with an odd number of occurrences of the substring ab we first construct an expression w defining strings over $\{a, b, c\}$ that do not contain the substring ab.

$$w = b^*(a \cup cb^*)^*$$

Using w, the desired set can be written $(wabwab)^*wabw$.

26. a) $\begin{aligned}
(ba)^+(a^*b^* \cup a^*) &= (ba)^+(a^*)(b^* \cup \lambda) \quad \text{'identity 5'} \\
&= (ba)^*baa^*(b^* \cup \lambda) \quad \text{'identity 4'} \\
&= (ba)^*ba^+(b^* \cup \lambda)
\end{aligned}$

Chapter 3

Context-Free Grammars

1. a)

derivation	rule
$S \Rightarrow abSc$	$S \rightarrow abSc$
$\Rightarrow ababScc$	$S \rightarrow abSc$
$\Rightarrow ababAcc$	$S \rightarrow A$
$\Rightarrow ababcAdcc$	$A \rightarrow cAd$
$\Rightarrow ababccddcc$	$A \rightarrow cd$

b)

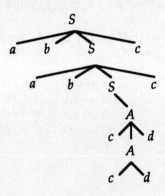

c) $L(G)= \{(ab)^n c^m d^m c^n \mid n \geq 0, m > 0\}$

3. a)
$$
\begin{aligned}
S &\Rightarrow AB \\
&\Rightarrow aAB \\
&\Rightarrow aaB \\
&\Rightarrow aaAB \\
&\Rightarrow aaaB \\
&\Rightarrow aaab
\end{aligned}
$$

b)
$$
\begin{aligned}
S &\Rightarrow AB \\
&\Rightarrow AAB \\
&\Rightarrow AAb \\
&\Rightarrow Aab \\
&\Rightarrow aAab \\
&\Rightarrow aaab
\end{aligned}
$$

c) There are 20 derivations that generate DT.

5. a) The S rules $S \rightarrow aaSB$ and $S \rightarrow \lambda$ generate an equal number of leading aa's and trailing B's. Each B is transformed into one or more b's. Thus the language of the grammar is $\{(aa)^i b^j \mid i \geq 0, j \geq i\}$.

c) The S rules $S \rightarrow aS$ and $S \rightarrow bS$ generate any combination of a's and b's. The rules $S \rightarrow A$ and $A \rightarrow cA$ then allow the generation of any number of c's. Eventually, the A is replaced by S allowing the entire sequence to be repeated or is transformed into c terminating the derivation. Thus, these rules generate $\{(\{a,b\}^{i_k} c^{j_k})^k c \mid i_k \geq 0, j_k \geq 0, k \geq 0\}$.

11. The language $a(a \cup c)^* b(a \cup c)^* b(a \cup c)^* cc$ is generated by the regular grammar

$$
\begin{aligned}
S &\rightarrow aA \\
A &\rightarrow aA \mid cA \mid bB \\
B &\rightarrow aB \mid cB \mid bC \\
C &\rightarrow aC \mid cC \mid cD \\
D &\rightarrow c
\end{aligned}
$$

14. The language $(a \cup b)^*aa(a \cup b)^*bb(a \cup b)^*$ is generated by

$$G_1: S_1 \rightarrow aS_1 \mid bS_1 \mid aA$$
$$A \rightarrow aB$$
$$B \rightarrow aB \mid bB \mid bC$$
$$C \rightarrow bD$$
$$D \rightarrow aD \mid bD \mid \lambda$$

G_2 generates the strings $(a \cup b)^*bb(a \cup b)^*aa(a \cup b)^*$

$$G_2: S_2 \rightarrow aS_2 \mid bS_2 \mid bE$$
$$E \rightarrow bF$$
$$F \rightarrow aF \mid bF \mid aG$$
$$G \rightarrow aH$$
$$H \rightarrow aH \mid bH \mid \lambda$$

A grammar G that generates

$$(a \cup b)^*aa(a \cup b)^*bb(a \cup b)^* \cup (a \cup b)^*bb(a \cup b)^*aa(a \cup b)^*$$

can be obtained from G_1 and G_2. The rules of G consist of the rules of G_1 and G_2 augmented with $S \rightarrow S_1 \mid S_2$ where S is the start symbol of the composite grammar. The alternative S rules correspond to the $\cup$ in the definition of the language.

20. The language $((a \cup \lambda)b(a \cup \lambda))^*$ is generated by the grammar

$$S \rightarrow aA \mid bB \mid \lambda$$
$$A \rightarrow bB$$
$$B \rightarrow aS \mid S$$

This language consists of all strings over $\{a, b\}$ in which every a is preceded or followed by a b. An a generated by the rule $S \rightarrow aA$ is followed by a b. An a generated by $B \rightarrow aS$ is preceded by a b.

21. The objective is to construct a grammar that generates the set of strings over $\{a, b\}$ containing an even number of a's or an odd number of b's.

$$S \rightarrow E \mid O$$
$$E \rightarrow aX \mid bE \mid \lambda$$
$$X \rightarrow aE \mid bX$$
$$O \rightarrow bY \mid aO$$
$$Y \rightarrow aY \mid bO \mid \lambda$$

The E and X rules generate strings with an even number of a's and the O and Y rules generate strings with an odd number of b's.

25. The set of strings over $\{a, b, c\}$ that contain an odd number of occurrences of ab is generated by the grammar

$$S \to aA \mid bS \mid cS$$
$$A \to aA \mid bX \mid cS$$
$$X \to aY \mid bX \mid cX \mid \lambda$$
$$Y \to aY \mid bS \mid cX \mid \lambda$$

The sentential forms produced by these rules contain X and Y only when an odd number of ab's have been generated.

27. The language consisting of the set of strings $\{a^m b^n c^i \mid m > n + i\}$ is generated by

$$S \to aS \mid aA$$
$$A \to aAc \mid B$$
$$B \to aBb \mid \lambda$$

The S rules generate one or more leading a's. The rule $A \to aAc$ generates an equal number of a's and c's. Similarly, the rule $B \to aBb$ generates a's and b's.

32. Let G be the grammar $S \to aSbS \mid aS \mid \lambda$. We prove the more stringent condition, that every prefix of a sentential form of G has at least as many a's as b's. We will refer to this condition as the prefix property. The proof is by induction of the length of derivations of G.

basis: The strings $aSbS$, aS and λ are the only sentential forms produced by derivations of length one. The prefix property is seen to hold for these strings by inspection.

inductive hypothesis: Assume that every sentential form that can be obtained by a derivation of length n or less satisfies the prefix property.

inductive step: Let w be a sentential form of G that can be derived using $n + 1$ rule applications. The derivation of w can be written

$$S \overset{n}{\Rightarrow} uSv \Rightarrow w$$

where w is obtained by applying an S rule to uSv. By the inductive hypothesis uSv satisfies the prefix property. A prefix of w consists of a prefix of uSv with the S replaced by λ, aS or $aSbS$. Thus w also satisfies the prefix property.

38. A regular grammar is one with rules of the form $A \to aB$, $A \to a$ and $A \to \lambda$ where $A, B \in V$ and $a \in \Sigma$. The rules of a right-linear grammar have the form $A \to \lambda$, $A \to u$ and $A \to uB$ where $A, B \in V$ and $u \in \Sigma^+$. Since every regular grammar is also right-linear, all regular languages are generated by right-linear grammars.

We now must show that every language generated by a right-linear grammar is regular. Let G be a right-linear grammar. A regular grammar G' that generates L(G) is constructed from the rules of G. Rules of the form $A \to aB$, $A \to a$ and $A \to \lambda$ in G are also in G'. A right-linear rule $A \to a_1 \dots a_n$ with $n > 1$ is transformed into a sequence of rules

$$A \to a_1 T_1$$
$$T_1 \to a_2 T_2$$
$$\vdots$$
$$T_{n-1} \to a_n$$

where the T_i's are variables not occurring in G. The result of the application of the $A \to u$ of G is obtained by the derivation

$$A \Rightarrow a_1 T_1 \Rightarrow \cdots \Rightarrow a_1 \dots a_{n-1} T_{n-1} \Rightarrow a_1 \dots a_n$$

in G'. This procedure is repeated for every rule $A \to u$. Similarly, rules of the form $A \to uB$, $length(u) > 1$, can be transformed into a sequence of rules of the form $A \to aC$. Clearly, the grammar G' constructed in this manner generates L(G).

Chapter 4

Parsing: An Introduction

3. a) Repeated applications of the rule $S \rightarrow SS$ produces sentential forms consisting of a positive number of S's. Each S derives a string in a^+b^+. Thus $L(G) = (a^+b^+)^+$.

b) The rules $S \rightarrow aS$ and $S \rightarrow Sb$ allow the generation of leading a's or trailing b's in any order. Two leftmost derivations for the string $aabb$ are

$$
\begin{aligned}
S &\Rightarrow aS & S &\Rightarrow Sb \\
&\Rightarrow aSb & &\Rightarrow aSb \\
&\Rightarrow aabb & &\Rightarrow aabb
\end{aligned}
$$

c) The derivation trees corresponding to the derivations of b) are

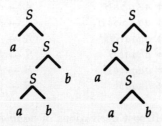

d) The equivalent unambiguous regular grammar

$$
\begin{aligned}
S &\rightarrow aS \mid aA \\
A &\rightarrow bA \mid bS \mid b
\end{aligned}
$$

generates strings in $L(G)$ in a left-to-right manner. The S rules generate the a's and the A rules generate the b's. The process is repeated by the application of the rule $A \rightarrow bS$.

15

7 a) L(G) is the set $\{\lambda\} \cup \{a^i b^j \mid i > 1, j > 0\}$. The null string is generated directly by the rule $S \to \lambda$. The rule $S \to AaSbB$ generates one a and one b. Repeated applications of $S \to AaSbB$, $S \to \lambda$, $A \to aA$, and $B \to bB$ generate additional a's and b's. The rule $A \to a$ guarantees that there are two or more a's in every string in L(G).

b) To show that G is ambiguous we must find a string $w \in$ L(G) that can be generated by two distinct leftmost derivations. The prefix of a's can be generated either by applications of the rule $S \to AaSbB$ or by the A rules. Consider the derivation of the string $aaaabb$ in which two a's are generated by applications of the S rule.

derivation	rule
$S \Rightarrow AaSbB$	$S \to AaSbB$
$\Rightarrow AaAaSbBbB$	$S \to AaSbB$
$\Rightarrow aaAaSbBbB$	$A \to a$
$\Rightarrow aaaaSbBbB$	$A \to a$
$\Rightarrow aaaabBbB$	$S \to \lambda$
$\Rightarrow aaaabbB$	$B \to \lambda$
$\Rightarrow aaaabb$	$B \to \lambda$

The string can also be derived using the rules $A \to aA$ and $A \to a$ to generate the a's.

derivation	rule
$S \Rightarrow AaSbB$	$S \to AaSbB$
$\Rightarrow aAaSbB$	$A \to aA$
$\Rightarrow aaAaSbB$	$A \to aA$
$\Rightarrow aaaaSbB$	$A \to a$
$\Rightarrow aaaabB$	$S \to \lambda$
$\Rightarrow aaaabbB$	$B \to bB$
$\Rightarrow aaaabb$	$B \to \lambda$

The two distinct leftmost derivations of $aaaabb$ demonstrate the ambiguity of G.

c) The regular grammar

$$S \to aA \mid \lambda$$
$$A \to aA \mid aB$$
$$B \to bB \mid b$$

generates strings in L(G) in a left-to-right manner. The rules $S \rightarrow aA$ and $A \rightarrow aB$ guarantee the generation of at least two a's in every nonnull string. The rule $B \rightarrow b$, whose application terminates a derivation, ensures the presence of at least one b.

13. The search tree created by Algorithm 4.3.1 while parsing $((b))$ is given below. The nodes on each level are listed in the order of their generation.

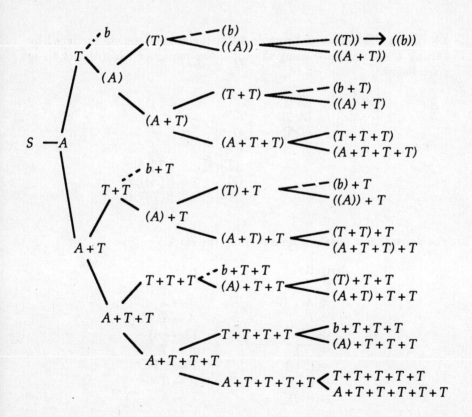

The derivation is obtained by following the arcs from the root S to the goal node $((b))$.

derivation	rule
$S \Rightarrow A$	$S \rightarrow A$
$\Rightarrow T$	$A \rightarrow T$
$\Rightarrow (A)$	$T \rightarrow (A)$
$\Rightarrow (T)$	$A \rightarrow T$
$\Rightarrow ((A))$	$T \rightarrow (A)$
$\Rightarrow ((T))$	$A \rightarrow T$
$\Rightarrow ((b))$	$T \rightarrow b$

14. Using the format of Example 4.4.1, the stack elements produced by parsing the string $((b))$ using the top-down parser of Algorithm 4.4.1 is given below.

~~$[S,0]$~~ $[S,1]$
          $[A,2]$
~~$[T,4]$~~ $[T,5]$
    b $[(A),2]$
          ~~$[(T),4]$~~ $[(T),5]$
            (b) $[((A)),2]$
                  $[((T)),4]$
                  $((b))$

The derivation is obtained directly from the stack.

derivation	rule
$S \Rightarrow A$	$S \rightarrow A$
$\Rightarrow T$	$A \rightarrow T$
$\Rightarrow (A)$	$T \rightarrow (A)$
$\Rightarrow (T)$	$A \rightarrow T$
$\Rightarrow ((A))$	$T \rightarrow (A)$
$\Rightarrow ((T))$	$A \rightarrow T$
$\Rightarrow ((b))$	$T \rightarrow b$

19. The parse of string $(b))$ is given using the bottom-up parser of Algorithm 4.6.1 in the format of Example 4.6.1.

stack	u	i	v	operation
$[\lambda, 0, (b))]$	-	-	-	-
-	λ	0	$(b))$	pop
-	$($	0	$b))$	shift
-	$(b$	0	$))$	shift
$[(b, 4,))]$	$(T$	0	$))$	reduction
$[(T, 2,))]$ $[(b, 4,))]$	$(A$	0	$))$	reduction
$[(T, 2,))]$ $[(b, 4,))]$	(A)	0	$)$	shift
$[(A), 5,)]$ $[(T, 2,))]$ $[(b, 4,))]$	T	0	$)$	reduction
$[T, 2,)]$ $[(A), 5,)]$ $[(T, 2,))]$ $[(b, 4,))]$	A	0	$)$	reduction
$[T, 2,)]$ $[(A), 5,)]$ $[(T, 2,))]$ $[(b, 4,))]$	$A)$	0	λ	shift
$[(A), 5,)]$ $[(T, 2,))]$ $[(b, 4,))]$	T	2	$)$	pop
$[(A), 5,)]$ $[(T, 2,))]$ $[(b, 4,))]$	$T)$	0	λ	shift

$[(T,2,)]$					
$[(b,4,)]$	(A)	5	)		pop
$[(T,2,)]$					
$[(b,4,)]$	$(A))$	0	λ		shift
$[(b,4,)]$	$(T$	2	))		pop
$[(b,4,)]$	(T)	2	)		shift
$[(b,4,)]$	$(T))$	2	λ		shift
-	$(b$	4	))		pop
-	(b)	0	)		shift
-	$(b))$	0	λ		shift

rejects

21. Algorithm 4.6.1 will not terminate when run with input string aa and grammar

$$S \rightarrow A \mid a \mid aa$$
$$A \rightarrow S$$

The rule $S \rightarrow a$ establishes Sa as the result of the first reduction for the string aa. The parse proceeds by alternating reductions with the rule $A \rightarrow S$ and the rule $S \rightarrow A$.

Chapter 5

Normal Forms

3. An equivalent essentially noncontracting grammar G_L with a nonrecursive start symbol is constructed following the steps given in the proof of Theorem 5.1.5. The start symbol of G_L is S_L. Because $\lambda \in L(G)$, $S_L \rightarrow \lambda$ is a rule of G_L. The set of nullable variables of G is $\{S, A, B\}$. All possible derivations of λ from these variables are eliminated by the addition of five S rules, one A rule, and one B rule. The resulting grammar is

$$
\begin{aligned}
S_L &\rightarrow S \mid \lambda \\
S &\rightarrow BSA \mid BS \mid SA \mid BA \mid B \mid S \mid A \\
A &\rightarrow aA \mid a \\
B &\rightarrow Bba \mid ba
\end{aligned}
$$

7. Algorithm 5.2.1 is used to determine the variables derivable using only chain rules.

$$
\begin{aligned}
\text{CHAIN}(S) &= \{S, A, B, C\} \\
\text{CHAIN}(A) &= \{A, B, C\} \\
\text{CHAIN}(B) &= \{B, C, A\} \\
\text{CHAIN}(C) &= \{C, A, B\}
\end{aligned}
$$

These sets are used to generate the rules of G_C according to the technique of Theorem 5.2.3, resulting in the grammar

$$
\begin{aligned}
S &\rightarrow aa \mid bb \mid cc \\
A &\rightarrow aa \mid bb \\
B &\rightarrow bb \mid cc \\
C &\rightarrow cc \mid aa
\end{aligned}
$$

21

In the grammar obtained by this transformation, it is clear that the A, B, and C rules do not contribute to derivations of terminal strings.

12. An equivalent grammar G_U without useless symbols is constructed in two steps. The first step involves the construction of a grammar G_T all of whose variables derive terminal strings. Algorithm 5.3.2 is used to construct the set TERM of variables that derive terminal strings.

Iteration	TERM	PREV
0	$\{D, F, G\}$	-
1	$\{D, F, G, A\}$	$\{D, F, G\}$
2	$\{D, F, G, A, S\}$	$\{D, F, G, A\}$
3	$\{D, F, G, A, S\}$	$\{D, F, G, A, S\}$

G_T is obtained by deleting all rules with variables in V − TERM.

$$V_T = \{S, A, D, F, G\}$$
$$\Sigma_T = \{a, b\}$$
$$P_T :\ S \rightarrow aA$$
$$A \rightarrow aA \mid aD$$
$$D \rightarrow bD \mid b$$
$$F \rightarrow aF \mid aG \mid a$$
$$G \rightarrow a \mid b$$

The second step in the construction of G_U involves the removal of all variables from G_T that are not reachable from S. Algorithm 5.3.4 is used to construct the set REACH of variables reachable from S.

Iteration	REACH	PREV	NEW
0	$\{S\}$	ϕ	-
1	$\{S, A\}$	$\{S\}$	$\{S\}$
2	$\{S, A, D\}$	$\{S, A\}$	$\{A\}$
3	$\{S, A, D\}$	$\{S, A, D\}$	$\{D\}$

Removing all references to variables in the set V_T − REACH produces the grammar

$$V_U = \{S, A, D\}$$
$$\Sigma_U = \{a, b\}$$
$$P_U :\ S \rightarrow aA$$
$$A \rightarrow aA \mid aD$$
$$D \rightarrow bD \mid b$$

15. To convert G to Chomsky normal form, we begin by transforming the rules of G to the form $S \to \lambda$, $A \to a$, or $A \to w$ where w is a string consisting solely of variables.

$$S \to XAYB \mid ABC \mid a$$
$$A \to XA \mid a$$
$$B \to YBZC \mid b$$
$$C \to XYZ$$
$$X \to a$$
$$Y \to b$$
$$Z \to c$$

The transformation is completed by breaking each rule whose right-hand side has length greater than 2 into a sequence of rules of the form $A \to BC$.

$$S \to XT_1 \mid AT_3 \mid a$$
$$T_1 \to AT_2$$
$$T_2 \to YB$$
$$T_3 \to BC$$
$$A \to XA \mid a$$
$$B \to YT_4 \mid b$$
$$T_4 \to BT_5$$
$$T_5 \to ZC$$
$$C \to XT_6$$
$$T_6 \to YZ$$
$$X \to a$$
$$Y \to b$$
$$Z \to c$$

22. The transformation of a grammar G from Chomsky normal form to Greibach normal form is accomplished in two phases. In the first phase, the variables of the grammar are numbered and an intermediate grammar is constructed in which the first symbol of the right-hand side of every rule is either a terminal or a variable with a higher number. This is done by removing direct left recursion and by applying the rule replacement schema of Lemma 5.6.2. The variables S, A, B, and C are numbered 1, 2, 3, and 4, respectively. The S rules are already in the proper form. Removing direct left recursion from the A rules produces the grammar

$$S \to AB \mid BC$$
$$A \to aR_1 \mid a$$
$$B \to AA \mid CB \mid b$$
$$C \to a \mid b$$
$$R_1 \to BR_1 \mid B$$

Applying the rule transformation schema of Lemma 5.6.2, the rule $B \rightarrow AA$ can be converted into the desired form by substituting for the first A, resulting in the grammar

$$S \rightarrow AB \mid BC$$
$$A \rightarrow aR_1 \mid a$$
$$B \rightarrow aR_1A \mid aA \mid CB \mid b$$
$$C \rightarrow a \mid b$$
$$R_1 \rightarrow BR_1 \mid B$$

The second phase consists of transformating the rules of the intermediate grammar to ensure that the first symbol of the right-hand side of each rule is a terminal symbol. Working backwards from the C rules and applying Lemma 5.6.2, we obtain

$$S \rightarrow aR_1B \mid AB \mid aR_1AC \mid aAC \mid aBC \mid bBC \mid bC$$
$$A \rightarrow aR_1 \mid a$$
$$B \rightarrow aR_1A \mid aA \mid aB \mid bB \mid b$$
$$C \rightarrow a \mid b$$
$$R_1 \rightarrow BR_1 \mid B$$

The same strategy is used to rewrite the R_1 rules, producing the Greibach normal form grammar

$$S \rightarrow aR_1B \mid AB \mid aR_1AC \mid aAC \mid aBC \mid bBC \mid bC$$
$$A \rightarrow aR_1 \mid a$$
$$B \rightarrow aR_1A \mid aA \mid aB \mid bB \mid b$$
$$C \rightarrow a \mid b$$
$$R_1 \rightarrow aR_1AR_1 \mid aAR_1 \mid aBR_1 \mid bR_1 \mid aR_1A \mid aA \mid aB \mid bB \mid b$$

Chapter 6

Finite Automata

1. a) The state diagram of M is

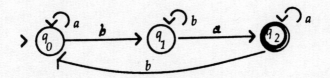

b) *i)*

$\vdash$ $[q_0, abaa]$
$\vdash$ $[q_0, baa]$
$\vdash$ $[q_1, aa]$
$\vdash$ $[q_2, a]$
$\vdash$ $[q_2, \lambda]$

ii)

$[q_0, bbbabb]$
$\vdash$ $[q_1, bbabb]$
$\vdash$ $[q_1, babb]$
$\vdash$ $[q_1, abb]$
$\vdash$ $[q_2, bb]$
$\vdash$ $[q_0, b]$
$\vdash$ $[q_1, \lambda]$

iii)

$[q_0, bababa]$
$\vdash$ $[q_1, ababa]$
$\vdash$ $[q_2, baba]$
$\vdash$ $[q_0, aba]$
$\vdash$ $[q_0, ba]$
$\vdash$ $[q_1, a]$
$\vdash$ $[q_2, \lambda]$

iv)

$[q_0, bbbaa]$
$\vdash$ $[q_1, bbaa]$
$\vdash$ $[q_1, baa]$
$\vdash$ $[q_1, aa]$
$\vdash$ $[q_2, a]$
$\vdash$ $[q_2, \lambda]$

c) The computations in *i*, *iii*, and *iv* terminate in the accepting state q_2. Therefore, the strings *abaa*, *bababa*, and *bbbaa* are in L(M).

d) Two regular expressions describing L(M) are $a^*b^+a^+(ba^*b^+a^+)^*$ and $(a^*b^+a^+b)^*a^*b^+a^+$.

4. A DFA that accepts the strings over $\{a, b\}$ that do not contain the substring aaa is given by the state diagram below.

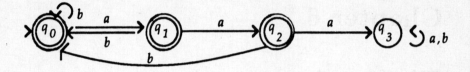

The states are used to count the number of consecutive a's that have been processed. When three consecutive a's are encountered, the DFA enters state q_3, processes the remainder of the input, and rejects the string.

9. The DFA

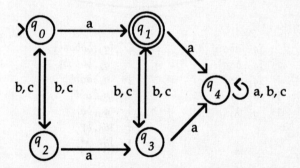

accepts strings of odd length over $\{a, b, c\}$ that contain exactly one a. A string accepted by this machine must have exactly one a and the total number of b's and c's must be even. A computation that processes an even number of b's and c's terminates in state q_0 or q_1. States q_1 or q_3 are entered upon processing a single a. The state q_1 represents the combination of the two conditions required for acceptance.

13. b) The NFA

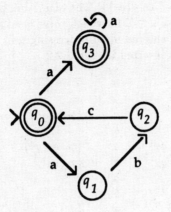

accepts the language $(abc)^*a^*$. Strings of the form $(abc)^*$ are accepted in q_0. State q_3 accepts $(abc)^*a^+$.

18. The set of strings over $\{a, b\}$ whose third to the last symbol is b is accepted by the NFA

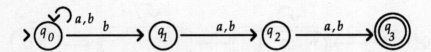

Nondeterminism is used to choose whether to enter state q_1 when processing a b in state q_0. If q_1 is entered upon processing the third to the last symbol, the computation accepts the input. A computation that enters q_1 in any other manner terminates unsuccessfully.

24. Algorithm 6.6.3 is used to construct a DFA that is equivalent to the NFA M in Example 12 a). Since M does not contain λ-transitions, the input transition function used by the algorithm is the transition function of M.

δ	a	b
q_0	$\{q_0, q_1, q_2\}$	ϕ
q_1	ϕ	$\{q_1, q_2\}$
q_2	$\{q_1\}$	ϕ

The set of nodes Q' of the equivalent NFA is constructed in step 2 of the algorithm. Q' is initialized to $\{\{q_0\}\}$. The algorithm proceeds by choosing a state $X \in Q'$ and symbol $u \in \Sigma$ for which there is no arc leaving X labeled u. The set Y is the state entered upon processing u in state X. If the set Y is not already in Q', it is inserted in step 2.2.2.

X	a	Y
$\{q_0\}$	a	$\{q_0, q_1, q_2\}$
$\{q_0\}$	b	ϕ
$\{q_0, q_1, q_2\}$	a	$\{q_0, q_1, q_2\}$
$\{q_0, q_1, q_2\}$	b	$\{q_1, q_2\}$
ϕ	a	ϕ
ϕ	b	ϕ
$\{q_1, q_2\}$	a	$\{q_1\}$
$\{q_1, q_2\}$	b	$\{q_1, q_2\}$
$\{q_1\}$	a	ϕ
$\{q_1\}$	b	$\{q_1, q_2\}$

Upon completion, Q' is the set $\{\{q_0\}, \{q_0, q_1, q_2\}, \phi, \{q_1, q_2\}, \{q_1\}\}$. The accepting states are $\{q_0, q_1, q_2\}$ and $\{q_1, q_2\}$. The state diagram of the deterministic machine is

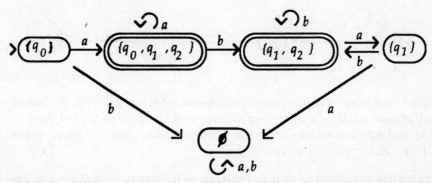

26. a) A regular expression is obtained by deleting nodes from the expression graphs

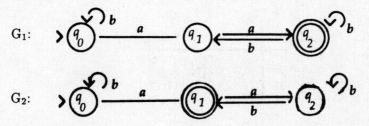

Deleting q_1 from G_1 produces

with the corresponding regular expression $b^*aa(ba \cup b)^*$. Removing q_2 from G_2 we obtain

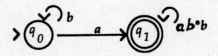

generating $b^*a(ab^*b)^*$. Consequently, the original NFA accepts strings of the form $b^*aa(ba \cup b)^* \cup b^*a(ab^*b)^*$.

Chapter 7

Regular Languages and Sets

2. b) To show that the set P of even length palindromes is not regular, it suffices to find strings u_i and v_i that satisfy

i) $u_i v_i \in P$

ii) $u_i v_j \notin P$ whenever $i \neq j$.

Let $u_i = a^i b$ and $v_i = ba^i$. Then $u_i v_i$ is the palindrome $a^i bba^i$. For $i \neq j$, the string $u_i v_j = a^i bba^j$ is not in P. We conclude, by Corollary 7.2.2, that P is not regular.

3. b) Assume that $L = \{a^n b^m \mid n < m\}$ is regular. Let k be the number specified by the pumping lemma and z be the string $a^k b^{k+1}$. This implies that z can be written uvw where

i) $v \neq \lambda$

ii) $length(uv) \leq k$

iii) $uv^i w \in L$ for all $i \geq 0$.

By condition *iii*, v consists solely of a's. Pumping v produces the string $uv^2 w$ that contains at least as many a's as b's. Thus $uv^2 w \notin L$ and L is not regular.

5. a) Let L be a regular language and L' the language consisting of all strings over $\{a, b, c\}$ that contain an a. L' is regular since it is defined by the regular expression $(a \cup b \cup c)^* a (a \cup b \cup c)^*$. The set

$$L \cap L' = \{w \mid w \in L \text{ and } w \text{ contains an } a\}$$

31

is regular by Theorem 7.4.3.

6. b) Let L_1 be a nonregular language and L_2 be a finite language. Assume that $L_1 - L_2$ is regular. Since every finite language is regular, we may use the closure properties of regular languages to combine $L_1 - L_2$ and L_2. By Theorem 7.4.1,

$$L_1 = (L_1 - L_2) \cup L_2$$

is regular. But this is a contradiction, and we conclude that $L_1 - L_2$ is not regular.

7. a) Let $G = (V, \Sigma, S, P)$ be a regular grammar that generates L. Without loss of generality, we may assume that G does not contain useless symbols. The algorithm to remove useless symbols, presented in Section 5.3, does not alter the form of rules of the grammar. Thus the equivalent grammar obtained by this transformation is also regular.

Derivations in G have the form $S \overset{*}{\Rightarrow} uA \overset{*}{\Rightarrow} uv$ where $u, v \in \Sigma^*$. A grammar G' that generates $P = \{u \mid uv \in L\}$ (the set of prefixes of L) can be constructed by augmenting the rules of G with rules $A \to \lambda$ for every variable $A \in V$. The prefix u is produced by the derivation $S \overset{*}{\Rightarrow} uA \Rightarrow u$ in G'.

9. a) The regular languages over a set Σ are constructed using the operations union, concatenation and Kleene star. We begin by showing that these set operations are preserved by homomorphisms. That is, for sets X and Y and homomorphism h

i) $h(XY) = h(X)h(Y)$

ii) $h(X \cup Y) = h(X) \cup h(Y)$

iii) $h(X^*) = h(X)^*$.

The set equality $h(XY) = h(X)h(Y)$ can be obtained by establishing the inclusions $h(XY) \subseteq h(X)h(Y)$ and $h(X)h(Y) \subseteq h(XY)$.

Let x be an element of $h(XY)$. Then $x = h(uv)$ for some $u \in X$ and $v \in Y$. Since h is a homomorphism, $x = h(u)h(v)$ and $x \in h(X)h(Y)$. Thus $h(XY) \subseteq h(X)h(Y)$. To establish the opposite inclusion, let x be an element in $h(X)h(Y)$. Then $x = h(u)h(v)$ for some $u \in X$ and $v \in Y$. As before, $x = h(uv)$ and $h(X)h(Y) \subseteq h(XY)$. The other two set equalities can be established by similar arguments.

Now let Σ_1 and Σ_2 be languages and h a homomorphism from Σ_1^* to Σ_2^*. We will use the regular set construction of regular languages to show that $h(X)$ is regular whenever X is. The proof is by induction on the number of operations in the definition of X.

basis: The basis consists of all regular sets over Σ_1 that are defined using no operations. These consist of $\emptyset$, $\{\lambda\}$, and $\{a\}$ for every $a \in \Sigma_1$. The homomorphic images of these sets are the regular sets $\emptyset$, $\{\lambda\}$ and $\{h(a)\}$, respectively.

inductive hypothesis: Now assume that the homomorphic image of every regular set definable using n or fewer operations is regular.

inductive step: Let X be a set definable by $n+1$ operations. Then X can be written $Y \cup Z$, YZ, or Y^* where Y and Z are definable by n or fewer operations. By the inductive hypothesis, $h(Y)$ and $h(Z)$ are regular. It follows that $h(X)$ is also regular.

11. The following Lemma establishes a relationship between regular and left-regular grammars.

Lemma. For every regular grammar $G = (V, \Sigma, S, P)$ there is a corresponding a left-regular grammar $G' = (V, \Sigma, S, P')$, defined by

i) $A \rightarrow Ba \in P'$ if, and only if, $A \rightarrow aB \in P$

ii) $A \rightarrow a \in P'$ if, and only if, $A \rightarrow a \in P$

iii) $A \rightarrow \lambda \in P'$ if, and only if, $A \rightarrow \lambda \in P$.

Let G and G' by corresponding regular and left-regular grammars. Then $L(G') = L(G)^R$.

The lemma can be proven by showing that $S \overset{*}{\Rightarrow} u$ in G if, and only if, $S \overset{*}{\Rightarrow} u^R$ in G'. The proof is by induction on the length of the derivations. The construction establishes a one-to-one correspondence between regular and left-regular grammars.

a) Let L be a language generated by a left-regular grammar G'. By the preceding lemma, the corresponding regular grammar G generates L^R. Since regularity is preserved by the operation of reversal, $(L^R)^R = L$ is regular. Thus every language generated by a left-regular grammar is regular.

b) Now we must show that every regular language is generated by a left-regular grammar. If L is a regular language, then so is L^R. This implies that there is a regular grammar G that generates L^R. The corresponding left-regular grammar G' generates $(L^R)^R = L$.

Chapter 8

Pushdown Automata

1. a) The PDA M accepts the language $\{a^i b^j \mid i \geq j\}$. Processing an a pushes A onto the stack. Strings of the form a^i are accepted in state q_1. The transitions in q_1 empty the stack after the input has been read. A computation with input $a^i b^j$ enters state q_2 upon processing the first b. To read the entire input string, the stack must contain at least j b's. The transition $\delta(q_2, \lambda, A) = [q_2, \lambda]$ will pop any A's remaining on the stack.

c) To show that the strings $aabb$ and $aaab$ are in the language of M, we exhibit a computation that accepts these strings.

state	string	stack
q_0	$aabb$	λ
q_0	abb	A
q_0	bb	AA
q_2	b	A
q_2	λ	λ

state	string	stack
q_0	$aaab$	λ
q_0	aab	A
q_0	ab	AA
q_0	b	AAA
q_2	λ	AA
q_2	λ	A
q_2	λ	λ

Both of these computations terminate in the accepting state q_2 with an empty stack.

3. d) The pushdown automaton defined by the transitions

$$\delta(q_0, \lambda, \lambda) = \{[q_1, C]\}$$
$$\delta(q_1, a, A) = \{[q_2, A]\}$$
$$\delta(q_1, a, C) = \{[q_2, C]\}$$
$$\delta(q_1, b, B) = \{[q_3, B]\}$$
$$\delta(q_1, b, C) = \{[q_3, C]\}$$
$$\delta(q_1, a, B) = \{[q_1, \lambda]\}$$
$$\delta(q_1, b, A) = \{[q_1, \lambda]\}$$
$$\delta(q_1, \lambda, C) = \{[q_4, \lambda]\}$$
$$\delta(q_2, \lambda, \lambda) = \{[q_1, A]\}$$
$$\delta(q_3, \lambda, \lambda) = \{[q_1, B]\}$$

accepts the strings that have the same number of a's and b's. A computation begins by pushing a C onto the stack. The stack is used to record the difference in the number of a's and b's scanned during the computation. The stack will contain n A's if the automaton has processed n more a's than b's. Similarly, the number of B's on the stack indicates the number of b's in excess of the number of a's that have been processed.

When an a is read with an A or C on the top of the stack, an A is pushed onto the stack. This is accomplished by the transition to q_2. If a B is on the top of the stack, the stack is popped since reading the a decreases the difference between the number of b'a and a's that have been processed. A similar strategy is employed when the computation reads a b.

The lone accepting state of the automaton is q_4. If the input string has the same number of a's and b's, the transition to q_4 pops the C and terminates the computation.

3. i) The language L = $\{a^i b^j \mid i \leq j \leq 2 \cdot i\}$ is generated by the context-free grammar

$$S \rightarrow aSB \mid \lambda$$
$$B \rightarrow bb \mid b$$

The B rule generates one or two b's for each a. A pushdown automaton that accepts L uses the stack in a similar manner. Upon processing an a, the computation nondeterministically pushes one or two A's onto the stack.

$$\delta(q_0, a, \lambda) = \{[q_1, A]\}$$
$$\delta(q_0, \lambda, \lambda) = \{[q_3, \lambda]\}$$
$$\delta(q_0, a, \lambda) = \{[q_1, A]\}$$
$$\delta(q_0, b, A) = \{[q_2, \lambda]\}$$
$$\delta(q_1, \lambda, \lambda) = \{[q_0, A]\}$$
$$\delta(q_2, b, A) = \{[q_2, \lambda]\}$$

The states q_2 and q_3 are the accepting states of this machine. The null string is accepted in q_3. For a nonnull string $a^i b^j \in L$, one of the computations will push exactly j A's onto the stack. The stack is emptied by processing the b's in q_2.

12. a) Assume that language L consisting of strings over $\{a\}$ whose lengths are a perfect square is context-free language. By the pumping lemma, there is a number k such that every string in L with length k or more can be written $uvwxy$ where

i) $length(vwx) \leq k$

ii) v and x are not both null

iii) $uv^i wx^i y \in L$, for $i \geq 0$.

The string a^{k^2} must have a decomposition $uvwxy$ that satisfies the preceding conditions. Consider the length of the string $z = uv^2 wx^2 y$ obtained by pumping $uvwxy$.

$$
\begin{aligned}
length(z) &= length(uv^2 wx^2 y) \\
&= length(uvwxy) + length(u) + length(v) \\
&= k^2 + length(u) + length(v) \quad \text{by } i \quad \text{if } w\text{-}\epsilon \text{ th}_n) v\text{-}w x) = k\\
&\leq k^2 + k \\
&< (k+1)^2
\end{aligned}
$$

Since the length of z is greater than k^2 but less than $(k+1)^2$, we conclude that $z \notin L$ and that L is not context-free.

13. a) The language $L_1 = \{a^i b^{2 \cdot i} c^j \mid i, j \geq 0\}$ is generated by the context-free grammar

$$
\begin{aligned}
S &\to AC \\
A &\to aAbb \mid \lambda \\
C &\to cC \mid \lambda
\end{aligned}
$$

b) Similarly, $L_2 = \{a^j b^i c^{2 \cdot i} \mid i, j \geq 0\}$ is generated by

$$S \rightarrow AB$$
$$A \rightarrow aA \mid \lambda$$
$$B \rightarrow bBcc \mid \lambda$$

c) Assume $L_1 \cap L_2 = \{a^i b^{2 \cdot i} c^{4 \cdot i} \mid i \geq 0\}$ is context-free and let k be the number specified by the pumping lemma. The string $z = a^k b^{2 \cdot k} c^{4 \cdot k}$ must admit a decomposition $uvwxy$ that satisfies the conditions of the pumping lemma. Because of the restriction on its length, the substring vwx must have the form a^i, b^i, c^i, $a^i b^j$, or $b^i c^i$. Pumping z produces the string $uv^2 wx^2 y$. This operation increases the number of at least one, possibly two, but not all three types of terminals in z. Thus $uv^2 wx^2 y \notin L$, contradicting the assumption that L is context-free.

22. b) Let $\Sigma = \{a, b, c\}$ and let $h : \Sigma^* \rightarrow \Sigma^*$ be the homomorphism obtained by using concatenation to extend the mapping $h(a) = a$, $h(b) = bb$, and $h(c) = ccc$ from elements of Σ to strings over Σ^*. The inverse image of $\{a^i b^{2 \cdot i} c^{3 \cdot i} \mid i \geq 0\}$ under the homomorphism h is $\{a^i b^i c^i \mid i \geq 0\}$. In Example 8.4.1, the pumping lemma was used to show that the latter language is not context-free. Since the class of context-free languages is closed under inverse homomorphic images (Exercise 21), it follows that $\{a^i b^{2 \cdot i} c^{3 \cdot i} \mid i \geq 0\}$ is not context-free.

Chapter 9

Turing Machines

1. a) $q_0 BaabcaB$
$\vdash Bq_1 aabcaB$
$\vdash Baq_1 abcaB$
$\vdash Baaq_1 bcaB$
$\vdash Baacq_1 caB$
$\vdash Baaccq_1 aB$
$\vdash Baaccaq_1 B$
$\vdash Baaccq_2 aB$
$\vdash Baacq_2 ccB$
$\vdash Baaq_2 cbcB$
$\vdash Baq_2 abbcB$
$\vdash Bq_2 acbbcB$
$\vdash q_2 BccbbcB$

b) $q_0 BbcbcB$
$\vdash Bq_1 bcbcB$
$\vdash Bcq_1 cbcB$
$\vdash Bccq_1 bcB$
$\vdash Bcccq_1 cB$
$\vdash Bccccq_1 B$
$\vdash Bcccq_2 cB$
$\vdash Bccq_2 cbB$
$\vdash Bcq_2 cbbB$
$\vdash Bq_2 cbbbB$
$\vdash q_2 BbbbbB$

c)

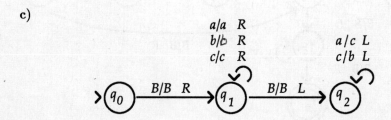

d) The result of a computation is to replace the a's in the input string with c's and the c's with b's.

3. a) Starting with the rightmost symbol in the input and working in a right-to-left manner, the machine diagrammed below moves each symbol one position to the right.

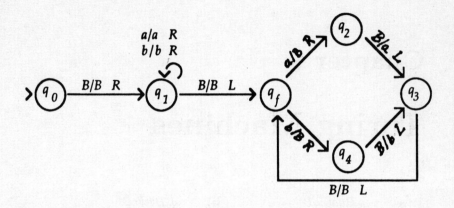

On reading the first blank following the input, the head moves to the left. If the input is the null string, the computation halts in state q_f with the tape head in position zero as desired. Otherwise, an a is moved to the right by transitions to states q_2 and q_3. Similarly, states q_4 and q_3 shift a b. This process is repeated until the entire string has been shifted.

6. c)

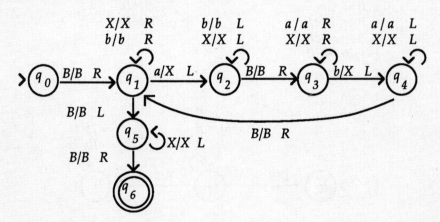

A computation begins by finding the first a on the tape and replacing it with an X (state q_1). The tape head is then returned to position zero and a search is initiated for a corresponding b. If a b is encountered, an X is written (state q_3) and the tape head is repositioned to repeat the cycle q_1, q_2, q_3, q_4. If no matching b is found, the computation halts in state q_3 rejecting the input. After all the a's have been processed, the entire string is read in q_1 and q_5 is entered upon reading the trailing blank. The computation halts in the accepting state q_6 if no b's remain on the tape.

8. Clearly, every recursively enumerable language is accepted by a Turing machine with stationary transitions. A standard Turing machine can be considered to be such a machine whose transition function does not include stationary transitions.

Let M be a Turing machine $(Q, \Sigma, \Gamma, \delta, q_0, F)$ with stationary transitions. We construct a standard Turing machine M' that accepts L(M). The transition function δ' of M' is constructed from that of M. A transition of M which is accompanied by a movement of the tape head generates an identical transition of M'.

i) $\delta'(q_i, x) = \delta(q_i, x)$ whenever $\delta(q_i, x) = [q_j, y, d]$ where $d \in \{L, R\}$

A pair of standard transitions are required to perform the same action as a stationary transition $\delta(x, q_i) = [q_j, y, S]$. The first transition prints a y, moves right and enters a new state. Regardless of the symbol being scanned, the subsequent transition moves left to the original position and enters q_j.

ii) $\delta'(q_i, x) = [q_t, y, R]$ for every transition $\delta(q_i, x) = [q_j, y, S]$ where $q_t \notin Q$ is a unique state. for every stationary transition

iii) $\delta'(q_t, z) = [q_j, z, L]$ for every $z \in \Gamma$ and q_t added in *ii*.

12. We refer to the method of acceptance defined in the problem as acceptance by entering. We show that the languages accepted by entering are precisely those accepted by final state, that is, the recursively enumerable languages.

Let $M = (Q, \Sigma, \Gamma, \delta, q_0, F)$ be a Turing machine that accepts by entering. The machine $M' = (Q, \Sigma, \Gamma, \delta', q_0, F)$ with transition function δ' defined by

i) $\delta'(q_i, x) = \delta(q_j, x)$ for all $q_i \notin F$

ii) $\delta'(q_i, x)$ is undefined for all $q_i \in F$

accepts L(M) be final state. Computations of M' are identical to those of M until M' enters an accepting state. When this occurs, M' halts, accepting the input. A computation of M that enters an accepting state halts in that state in M'.

Now let M = (Q, Σ, Γ, δ, q_0, F) be a Turing machine that accepts by final state. A computation of M may enter and leave accepting states prior to termination. The intermediate states have no bearing on the acceptance of the input. We construct a machine M' that accepts L(M) by entering. M' is defined by the quintuple (Q $\cup \{q_a\}$, Σ, Γ, δ', q_0, $\{q_a\}$). The transitions of M' are defined by

i) $\delta'(q_i, x) = \delta(q_i, x)$ whenever $\delta(q_i, x)$ is defined

ii) $\delta'(q_i, x) = [q_f, x, R]$ if $q_i \in$ F and $\delta(q_i, x)$ is undefined.

A computation of M that accepts an input string halts in an accepting state q_i. The computation of M' reaches q_i and then enters q_a, the lone accepting state of M'. Thus entering q_a in M' is equivalent to halting in an accepting state of M and L(M) = L(M').

13. b) The two-tape Turing machine with tape alphabet $\{a, b, B\}$ and accepting state is q_4 defined by the transitions

$$\delta(q_0, B, B) = [q_1; B, R; B, R]$$
$$\delta(q_1, x, B) = [q_1; x, R; x, R] \qquad \text{for every } x \in \{a, b\}$$
$$\delta(q_1, B, B) = [q_2; B, L; B, S]$$
$$\delta(q_2, x, B) = [q_2; x, L; B, S] \qquad \text{for every } x \in \{a, b\}$$
$$\delta(q_2, B, B) = [q_3; B, R; B, L]$$
$$\delta(q_3, x, x) = [q_3; x, R; x, L] \qquad \text{for every } x \in \{a, b\}$$
$$\delta(q_3, B, B) = [q_4; B, S; B, S]$$

accepts the palindromes over $\{a, b\}$. The input is copied onto tape two in state q_1. State q_2 returns the head reading tape one to the initial position. With tape head one moving left-to-right and head two moving right-to-left, the strings on the two tapes are compared. If both heads simultaneously read a blank, the computation terminates in q_4.

A computation requires precisely $3 \cdot n + 3$ transitions where n is the length of the input string. Tape head one, which moves with every transition, moves through the input three times. Each pass requires $n + 1$ transitions.

15. A deterministic machine M was constructed in Exercise 6 c) that accepts strings over $\{a, b\}$ with the same number of a's and b's. Using M, a composite machine is constructed to determine whether an input string contains a substring of length three or more with the same number of a's and b's. Nondeterminism is used to 'choose' a substring to be examined.

States p_0 to p_7 nondeterministically select a substring of length three or more from the input.

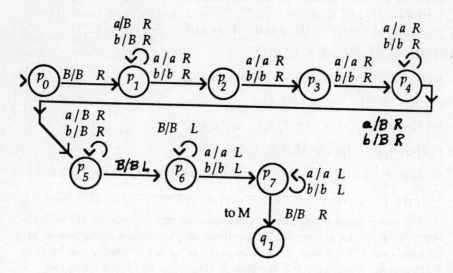

The transition to state q_1 of M begins the computation that checks whether the chosen substring has the same number of a's and b's. The accepting states of this submachine are the accepting states of M.

The computation of a deterministic machine generates a substring of the input and decides if it satisfies the conditions. If not, another substring is generated and examined. This process must be repeated until an acceptable substring is found or all substrings have been considered.

18. Let $M = (Q, \Sigma, \Gamma, \delta, q_0, F)$ be a Turing machine that demonstrates that L is a recursive language. Since every computation of M halts, the machine $(Q, \Sigma, \Gamma, \delta, q_0, Q - F)$ accepts the complement of L.

Conversely, we must show that L is recursive when both L and its complement are recursively enumerable. By Theorem 9.2.3, there are machines $M_1 = (Q_1, \Sigma, \Gamma_1, \delta_1, q_0)$ and $M_2 = (Q_2, \Sigma, \Gamma_2, \delta_2, p_0)$ that accept L and $\overline{L}$ by halting. These machines provide sufficient information to decide whether a string u is in L. If $u \in L$, then the computation of M_1 halts. On the other hand, if $u \notin L$ then M_2 halts.

We construct a two-tape machine M that simulates the computations of both M_1 and M_2. The input alphabet of M is Σ, the tape alphabet is $\Gamma_1 \cup \Gamma_2$ and the start state is r_0. A computation begins by copying the input onto tape two and repositioning the tape heads at the initial position. This is accomplished by the transitions defined in i through v. M then 'runs' M_1 on tape one and M_2 on tape two. The states of M that simulate the computation of the composite machines are elements of the Cartesian product $Q_1 \times Q_2 \times \{1, 2\}$. That is, a state is an ordered triple consisting of a state of M_1, a state of M_2 and an element of $\{1, 2\}$.

i) $\delta(r_0, B, B) = [r_1; B, R; B, R]$

ii) $\delta(r_1, x, B) = [r_1; x, R; x, R]$ for every $x \in \Sigma$

iii) $\delta(r_1, B, B) = [r_2; B, L; B, L]$

iv) $\delta(r_2, x, x) = [r_2; x, L; x, L]$ for every $x \in \Sigma$

v) $\delta(r_2, B, B) = [[q_0, p_0, 1]; B, S; B, S]$

vi) $\delta([q_i, p_j, 1], x, y) = [[q_n, p_j, 2]; s, d_1; y, S]$ whenever $\delta_1(q_i, x) = [q_n, s, d_1]$

vii) $\delta([q_i, p_j, 2], x, y) = [[q_i, p_m, 1]; x, S; t, d_2]$ whenever $\delta_2(p_j, y) = [p_n, t, d_2]$

For every input string, the computation of exactly one of M_1 and M_2 terminates. When a 1 occurs in the state, M processes a transition of M_1 on tape one. The status of the computation of M_2 is unaffected by such a transition. Similarly, a 2 specifies a transition of M_2 on tape two. A string is accepted if the computation halts due to the lack of a transition for a configuration on tape one. Thus the set of final states of M consists of triples of the form $[q_i, p_j, 1]$.

23.

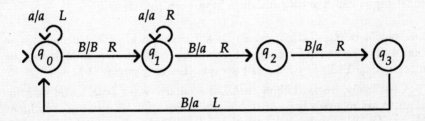

The cycle formed by states q_0, q_1, q_2, q_3 concatenates *aaa* to the right end of the string currently on the tape.

Chapter 10

The Chomsky Hierarchy

1. a) The unrestricted grammar

$$S \rightarrow X \mid Y \mid aPAbQb$$
$$X \rightarrow aaX \mid \lambda$$
$$Y \rightarrow bbY \mid \lambda$$
$$P \rightarrow aPA \mid \lambda$$
$$Q \rightarrow bQb \mid E$$
$$Ab \rightarrow bA$$
$$AE \rightarrow a$$
$$Aa \rightarrow aa$$

generates the language $\{a^i b^j a^i b^j \mid i,j \geq 0\}$. Rules $S \rightarrow X$ and $S \rightarrow Y$ initiate derivations that generate λ, a^{2i}, and b^{2i}. The derivation of a string $a^i b^j a^i b^j$, $i,j > 0$, begins with the rule $S \rightarrow aPAbQb$. Repeated applications of the P and Q rules produce $a^i A^i b^j E b^j$. The rules $Ab \rightarrow bA$, $AE \rightarrow a$, and $Aa \rightarrow aa$ are then used to obtain the desired configuration of the terminals. The derivation of $aabaab$ demonstrates the repositioning of the variable A and its transformation to the terminal a.

$$
\begin{aligned}
S &\Rightarrow aPAbQb \\
&\Rightarrow aaPAAbQb \\
&\Rightarrow aaAAbQb \\
&\Rightarrow aaAAbEb \\
&\Rightarrow aaAbAEb \\
&\Rightarrow aabAAEb \\
&\Rightarrow aabAab \\
&\Rightarrow aabaad
\end{aligned}
$$

3. Let $G = (V, \Sigma, P, S)$ be an unrestricted grammar. We construct a grammar $G' = (V', \Sigma, P', S)$ that generates $L(G)$ in which each rule has the form $u \to v$ where $u \in (V')^*$ and $v \in (V' \cup \Sigma)^*$. The set of variables of V' consists of the variables of V and a new variable T_a for every $a \in \Sigma$. For a string $u \in (V \cup \Sigma)^*$, let $T(u)$ denote the string obtained by replacing each terminal a in u with the corresponding variable T_a. The rules of G' are

i) $T(u) \to T(v)$ for every rule $u \to v \in P$

ii) $T_a \to a$ for every $a \in \Sigma$.

The grammar G contains a derivation $S \overset{*}{\Rightarrow} u$ if, and only if, $S \overset{*}{\Rightarrow} T(u)$ is a derivation of G'. Using the rules defined in *ii* to transform the variables T_a to the corresponding terminals, we see that $L(G) = L(G')$.

4. c) Let L_1 and L_2 be two recursively enumerable languages. We will construct an unrestricted grammar G that generates $L_1 L_2$ from grammars $G_1 = (V_1, \Sigma_1, P_1, S_1)$ and $G_2 = (V_2, \Sigma_2, P_2, S_2)$ that generate L_1 and L_2 respectively.

Let us first recall the proof of Theorem 8.5.1, which established that the context-free languages are closed under concatenation. The grammar

$$G = (V_1 \cup V_2, \Sigma_2 \cup \Sigma_2, P_1 \cup P_2 \cup \{S \to S_1 S_2\}, S)$$

was constructed from G_1 and G_2 where $S \notin V_1 \cup V_2$ and V_1 and V_2 are assumed to be disjoint. Unfortunately, we must be careful in combining unrestricted grammars in this manner since the left-hand side of a rule may contain more than one symbol. For example, consider derivations $S_1 \overset{*}{\Rightarrow} x$ in G_1 and $S_2 \overset{*}{\Rightarrow} y$ in G_2. It follows that $S \overset{*}{\Rightarrow} xy$. Now either P_1 or P_2 may contain a rule $u \to v$ where $xy = x'uy'$. In this case, the transformation obtained by the application of the rule $u \to v$ may produce a string that is not in the concatenation of L_1 and L_2.

The grammars G_1 and G_2 must be constructed to ensure that no rule can overlap the strings derived from S_1 and S_2. Using Exercise 3, we can assume that the left-hand side of every rule in G_1 and G_2 consists solely of variables. As before, we also assume that V_1 and V_2 are disjoint. When G_1 and G_2 satisfy these conditions, the grammar G defined above generates $L_1 L_2$.

7. Let L be a recursively enumerable language accepted by the Turing machine $M = (Q, \Sigma, \Gamma, \delta, q_0, F)$ and let c be a terminal symbol not in Σ. The language

$L' = \{ \, wc^i \mid M$ accepts w by a computation in which the tape
head does not read tape position $length(w) + i + 1\}$

is accepted by a linear-bounded machine M' constructed from M. The transitions of M' are identical to those of M except M' treats the c as a blank. If the computation of M' moves to the right of the sequence of c's, the computation halts rejecting the input.

12. Let $u \to v$ be a monotonic rule with $length(v) > 2$. We define a set P of monotonic rules that produce the same transformation as $u \to v$. The rules of P are constructed so that a string on the right-hand side of a rule has length less than $length(v)$. Without loss of generality we assume that $u, v \in V^*$. If not, every occurrence of a terminal a in u and v is replaced by a new variable T_a and the rule $T_a \to a$ is added to P. The construction of P is divided into two cases.

i) If $length(u) = 1$, then $u \to v$ can be written $A \to BCDv'$ where $A, B, C, D \in V$ and $v' \in V^*$. Using two new variables X and Y, the monotonic rules

$$A \to XY$$
$$X \to BC$$
$$Y \to Dv'$$

define the same transformation as $u \to v$.

ii) If $length(u) > 1$, then $u \to v$ can be written $AEu' \to BCDv'$. The rules

$$AE \to XY$$
$$X \to B$$
$$Yu' \to CDv'$$

generate the transformation $u \to v$.

In either case, the strings in the rules produced using these techniques have length at most $length(v) - 1$. This procedure can be repeated until the length of each string in the rules is at most two.

13. The string transformation obtained by applying the rule $AB \to CD$ can be obtained by the sequential application of the three rules

$$AB \to XB$$
$$XB \to XD$$
$$XD \to CD$$

Each of these rules has the context-sensitive form $uAv \to uwv$ with $w \neq \lambda$.

Chapter 11

Decidability

3. A nondeterministic two-tape Turing machine M is designed to solve the question of derivability in a regular grammar. A regular grammar $G = (V, \Sigma, P, S)$ has rules of the form $A \to aB$, $A \to a$ or $A \to \lambda$ where $A, B \in V$ and $a \in \Sigma$. A rule $A \to u$ is represented by the string Au. Rules are separated by the symbol #. The representation of a regular grammar, denoted $R(G)$, is the concatenation of the encoding of the rules. The input to M has the form $R(G)\#\#w$ where w is a string from Σ^*.

Consider the regular grammar G

$$S \to aS \mid aA \mid a$$
$$A \to bA \mid \lambda$$

that generates the language a^+b^* . The grammar G is represented by the string $SaS\#SaA\#Sa\#AbA\#A$. A computation of M to decide whether a string w is in L(G) begins with input $SaS\#SaA\#Sa\#AbA\#A\#\#w$.

The actions of a machine M that solves the derivability problem are described below. Tape two is used to simulate a derivation in G.

1. The computation of M begins by determining whether the input is the representation of a regular grammar followed by an input string. If not, M halts rejecting the input.

2. An S is written in position one of tape two.

3. Let uA be the string written on tape two. A rule $A \to v$ is chosen nondeterministically from the representation on tape one. The variable A is then replaced with v on tape two.

4. If v is a terminal symbol or the null string, the strings uv and w are compared. If they are identical, M halts and accepts the input. Otherwise, the input is rejected.

5. If $v = aB$ for some $a \in \Sigma$ and $B \in V$, then the lengths ua and w are compared. The input is rejected if $length(ua) = length(w)$. If not, Steps 3–5 are repeated.

Step 5 insures that a computation of M halts after at most $length(w)$ rule applications are simulated. Consequently, all computations of M terminate and M solves the derivability problem.

8. Let M be a Turing machine that accepts a nonrecursive language L. Without loss of generality, we may assume that a computation of M continues indefinitely for every string not in L.

Assume that there is a machine H that solves the halting problem for M. The halting machine H accepts a string w if M halts with input w. That is, if $w \in L$. Conversely, H halts and rejects all strings in $\overline{L}$. Consequently, $L(H) = L$. Since H halts for all input strings, it follows that L is recursive. This is a contradiction and we conclude that there is no halting machine H.

11. We will show that the halting problem is reducible to the question of whether a Turing machine enters a designated state. We begin by observing that the question of halting in a Turing machine M can be reduced to that of entering a particular state in a machine M'.

Let $M = (Q, \Sigma, \Gamma, \delta, q_0, F)$ be a Turing machine. The machine $M' = (Q \cup \{q_f\}, \Sigma, \Gamma, \delta', q_0, \{q_f\})$ with transition function

i) $\delta'(q_i, x) = \delta(q_i, x)$ whenever $\delta(q_i, x)$ is defined

ii) $\delta'(q_i, x) = [q_f, x, R]$ whenever $\delta(q_i, x)$ is undefined

accepts precisely the strings for which the computations of M halt. The computations of M' are identical to those of M until M halts. When this occurs, M' enters q_f.

Assume that there is a machine S that solves the state problem. The input to S is a representation of a Turing machine M, input string w and state q_i. S accepts the input if the computation of M with input w enters state q_i. Adding a preprocessor N to S, we construct a machine H that solves the halting problem.

The input to N is $R(M)w$, the representation of a Turing machine M followed by an input string. By adding the encoding of transitions to $R(M)$, N constructs the string $R(M')$. A machine H is constructed that

1. Runs N on input $R(M)w$ producing $R(M')w$.

2. Adds the encoding of q_f to the end of the input.

3. Runs S on the resulting string.

A computation of H accepts input $R(M)\#w$ if, and only if, M' enters state q_f when run with input w. That is, whenever M halts with input w. Steps 1 and 2 comprise a reduction of the halting problem to the state problem. We conclude that the machine S cannot exist and that the state problem is undecidable.

13. a) A solution to the Post correspondence system $\{[a, aa], [bb, b], [a, bb]\}$ is obtained by *playing* the dominoes

a	a	bb	bb
aa	bb	b	b

14. a) A solution to the Post correspondence system

$$\{[ab, a], [ba, bab], [b, aa], [ba, ab]\}$$

must begin with $[ab, a]$ or $[ba, bab]$ since these are the only pairs that have the same rightmost symbol. We will show that no sequence of dominoes can be constructed that solves this Post correspondence problem.

A domino that extends the sequence beginning with $[ab, a]$ must have a b as the first symbol in the bottom string. The only such ordered pair is $[ba, bab]$. Playing this produces

ab	ba
a	bab

in which the top and bottom strings differ in the third symbol.

There are three ways to extend a sequence that begins with $[ba, bab]$. Playing $[ba, bab]$ produces strings that disagree at the fourth position.

a)

ba	ba
bab	bab

b)

ba	b
bab	aa

c)

ba	ba
bab	ab

We now turn our attention to trying to extend sequence b). The next domino must have an a in the first position in the top string. Playing the only domino of this form we obtain the sequence

ba	b	ab
bab	aa	a

in which the strings disagree in the fifth position.

The only remaining candidate is sequence c). Note that the rightmost end of these strings has the same form as the sequence consisting solely of the domino $[ba, bab]$. That is, the length of the bottom string is one greater than that of the top string with a b being the rightmost symbol on the bottom. The preceding argument can be repeated to show that

ba	ba	ba
bab	ab	ab

is the sole extension of c) that satisfies the conditions of a solution to this Post correspondence system.

The only way in which this sequence can be extended is to continually play $[ba, ab]$. Utilizing this strategy, the length of the top string is always one less than that of the bottom. It follows that there is no sequence of dominoes that comprises a solution to the Post correspondence system.

17. First we note that a Post correspondence problem C has infinitely many solutions whenever it is solvable. If w is the string spelled by a solution, then ww, www, ..., are also spelled by solutions. These solutions are obtained by repeating the sequence of dominoes that spell w.

Let C be a Post correspondence system and let G_U and G_V be the upper and lower grammars defined by C. By Theorem 11.7.1 we know that C has a solution if, and only if, $L(G_U) \cap L(G_V) \neq \emptyset$. Combining this with the previous observation, C having a solution is equivalent to $L(G_U)$ and $L(G_V)$ having infinitely many elements in common. It follows that there is no algorithm that can determine whether the intersection of the languages generated by two context-free grammars is an infinite set.

Chapter 12

Numeric Computation

2. d) The Turing machine M computes the relation

$$even(n) = \begin{cases} 1 & \text{if } n \text{ is even} \\ 0 & \text{otherwise.} \end{cases}$$

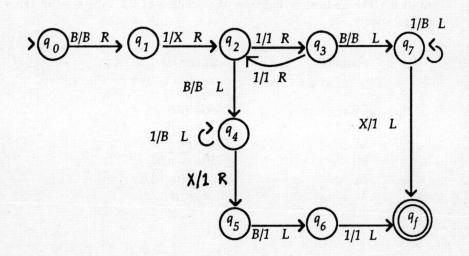

The input string represents an even number if a blank is read in q_2 and an odd number if a blank is read in q_3. After determining the parity, the input is erased and the appropriate output is written on the tape.

4. a) A machine can be constructed to compute the characteristic function of the greater than relation

$$gt(n, m) = \begin{cases} 1 & \text{if } n > m \\ 0 & \text{otherwise} \end{cases}$$

using the machine LT constructed in Exercise 3 f) to compute the less than function lt. The functions lt and gt satisfy the equality $gt(n, m) = lt(m, n)$.

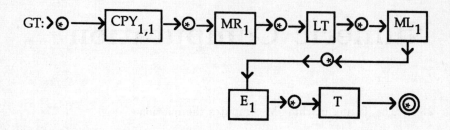

The action of the composite machine GT is exhibited by tracing a computation. The underscore indicates the position of the tape head in the configuration.

machine	configuration
	$B\underline{\overline{n}}B\overline{m}B$
$CPY_{1,1}$	$B\underline{\overline{n}}B\overline{m}B\overline{n}B$
MR_1	$B\overline{n}B\underline{\overline{m}}B\overline{n}B$
LT	$B\overline{n}B\underline{lt(m, n)}B$
ML_1	$B\underline{\overline{n}}Blt(m, n)B$
E_1	$\underline{B}\ldots Blt(m, n)B$
T	$B\underline{lt(m, n)}B$

7. Let f be a Turing computable function and F a machine that computes f. We construct a machine M that returns the first value for which $f(n) = 0$. A computation begins with $\overline{0}$ on the tape. The BRN macro is used to determine whether the value of f is 0. If not, the succeeding integer is written on the tape and its f value is computed. This loop continues until an integer n is encountered for which $f(n) = 0$.

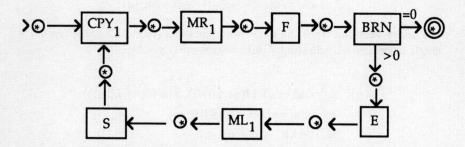

If f never assumes the value 0, the computation continues indefinitely. If f is not total, the computation will return the first value for which $f(n) = 0$ if $f(m)$ is defined for all $m < n$. Otherwise, M loops upon encountering the first value for which $f(m)\uparrow$.

10. Let R be a Turing computable unary relation and M a machine that computes the characteristic function of R. A machine that accepts R can be built using M and the branch macro.

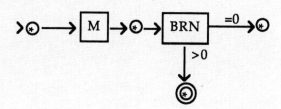

The computation of M halts with $\overline{0}$ on the tape if, and only if, the input string is not an element of R. Consequently, the composite machine accepts R.

13. a) The function

$$f = add \circ (mult \circ (id, id), \ add \circ (id, id))$$

is a unary function since the innermost functions (*id* in this case) require a
single argument. Evaluating f with argument n yields

$$
\begin{aligned}
f(n) &= add(mult(id(n), id(n)), add(id(n), id(n))) \\
&= add(mult(n, n), add(n, n)) \\
&= add(n \cdot n, n + n) \\
&= n^2 + 2 \cdot n
\end{aligned}
$$

Chapter 13

μ-Recursive Functions

2. b) The proper subtraction function $sub(x, y)$ was defined in Table 13.2.1 by

$$sub(x, 0) = x$$
$$sub(x, y + 1) = pred(sub(x, y))$$

where *pred* is the predecessor function. The functions $g = p_1^{(1)}$ and $h = pred \circ p_3^{(3)}$, built using the projection functions, the primitive recursive function *pred* and composition, formally define *sub*.

$$sub(x, 0) = g(x) = x$$
$$sub(x, y + 1) = h(x, y, sub(x, y)) = pred(sub(x, y))$$

4. d) The values of the predicate

$$even(y) = \begin{cases} 1 & \text{if } y \text{ is even} \\ 0 & \text{otherwise} \end{cases}$$

alternate between 0 and 1. The value of $even(y+1)$ can be obtained directly from $even(y)$ using the proper subtraction function.

$$even(0) = 1$$
$$even(y + 1) = 1 \dot{-} even(y)$$

The right-hand side of $even(y+1)$ uses only functions previously shown to be primitive recursive, the value $even(y)$, and composition. Consequently, *even* is also primitive recursive.

4. e) To define $half(y)$ using primitive recursion, we must determine the relationship between $half(y)$ and $half(y+1)$.

$$half(y+1) = \begin{cases} half(y) & \text{if } y+1 \text{ is odd} \\ half(y)+1 & \text{if } y+1 \text{ is even} \end{cases}$$

Translating this into the language of primitive recursion, we obtain the primitive recursive definition

$$half(0) = 0$$
$$half(y+1) = half(y) + even(y+1).$$

6. a) The two-variable predicate

$$f(x,y) = \begin{cases} 1 & \text{if } g(i) < g(x) \text{ for all } i \leq y \\ 0 & \text{otherwise} \end{cases}$$

is true only when the inequality $g(i) < g(x)$ is satisfied by every integer i between 0 and y. The bounded product

$$f(x,y) = \prod_{i=0}^{y} lt(g(i), g(x))$$

computes f using the primitive recursive function g. Since the family of primitive recursive functions is closed under bounded products, f is primitive recursive.

6. e) The bounded sum can be used to count the number of times $g(i) = x$ in the range $0 \leq i \leq y$.

$$n(x,y) = \sum_{i=0}^{y} eq(g(i), x)$$

The predicate $eq(g(i), x)$ is 1 only if $g(i) = x$. The summation records the number times this occurs in the designated range.

6. f) The function $n(x,y)$, defined above, is used to construct $thrd$. The first i that satisfies the predicate $eq(n(x,i), 3)$ is the third integer whose value $g(i)$ is x. Bounded minimalization is the primitive recursive tool for finding the first value that satisfies a predicate.

$$thrd(x,y) = ge(n(x,y), 3) \cdot \overset{y}{\mu}z \, [eg(n(x,z), 3)]$$

The factor $ge(n(x, y), 3)$ provides the default value whenever there are fewer than three integers in the range 0 to y for which g assumes the value x.

7. a) First we note that, by definition, no number is a divisor of 0. Thus, the greatest common divisor of 0 and any number is 0. Finding the greatest common divisor of x and y can be thought of as a search procedure. The objective is to find the greatest number less than or equal to x that divides both x and y. The predicate $divides(x, x \overset{.}{-} z) \cdot divides(y, x \overset{.}{-} z)$ is 1 whenever $x \overset{.}{-} z$ is a divisor of both x and y. The function

$$g(x, y) = \overset{x}{\mu} z \left[divides(x, x \overset{.}{-} z) \cdot divides(y, x \overset{.}{-} z) \right]$$

sequentially examines the predicates

$$divides(x, x) \cdot divides(y, x)$$
$$divides(x, x \overset{.}{-} 1) \cdot divides(y, x \overset{.}{-} 1)$$
$$divides(x, x \overset{.}{-} 2) \cdot divides(y, x \overset{.}{-} 2)$$
$$\vdots$$

The greatest common divisor can be obtained directly from g.

$$gcd(x, y) = sg(x) \cdot sg(y) \cdot (x \overset{.}{-} g(x, y))$$

The sg predicates handle the special case when one or both of the arguments are 0.

11. a) The prime decomposition of 18000 is $2^4 \cdot 3^2 \cdot 5^3$. This is a Gödel number since it consists of an initial sequence of the primes. The encoded sequence is 3, 1, 2.

12. a) The objective is to construct a primitive recursive one-variable predicate gdn whose value indicates whether the input is the encoding of a Gödel number. We begin by defining an auxiliary function

$$g(x) = \overset{x}{\mu} z \left[cosg(divides(x, pn(z))) \right]$$

that returns the number of the first prime that does not occur in the prime decomposition of x. If there are no primes greater than $pn(g(x))$ that divide x, then x is a Gödel number

Determining whether there is prime greater than $pn(g(x))$ occuring in the prime decomposition of x seems like it may require an unbounded search. However, we can determine if there are primes greater than $pn(g(x))$

that divide x by constructing the product of the powers of the primes less than $pn(g(x))$.

$$gdn(x) = eq(x, \prod_{i=0}^{g(x)-1} pn(i)^{dec(i,x)+1})$$

If the product equals x, then all the primes that divide x occur before $pn(g(x))$. In this case x is the encoding of a Gödel number. The equality predicate returns zero when there are primes greater than $pn(g(x))$ that divide x.

15. b) The value of the function $root(c_2, c_1, c_0)$ is the first nonnegative integer root of the quadratic equation $c_2 \cdot x^2 + c_1 \cdot x + c_0$. If there is no such root, $root(c_2, c_1, c_0)$ is undefined. The function

$$\mu z[eq(c_2 \cdot z^2 + c_1 \cdot z + c_0, 0)]$$

obtained using the unbounded μ-operator computes $root$.

Chapter 14

Computational Complexity

1. c) The length of the input of a Turing machine that computes a function of more than one variable is considered to be the length of the arguments plus the blanks that separate them. The Turing machine in Example 12.1.2 computes the binary function of string concatenation. The input has the form $BuBvB$ with length $length(u) + length(v) + 1$.

A computation moves through u and then shifts each element of v one position to the left. For an input of length n, the worst case number of transitions occurs when $u = \lambda$ and $length(v) = n - 1$. The values of of the trace function tr are given for the first four values of n.

n	$tr(n)$
1	4
2	8
3	12
4	16

The computation begins by reading the two blanks that precede v. Translating each symbol of v requires three transitions. The computation is completed by returning the tape head to the leftmost tape position. This requires $length(v) + 2$ transitions. Thus $tr(n) = 4 \cdot (n - 1) + 4 = 4 \cdot n$.

2. c) The function $f(n) = n^2 + 5 \cdot n + 2 + 10/n$ is obtained by multiplying the polynomials in the numerator and dividing each term by n^2. Intuitively, n^2 is the most significant contributor to the growth of f. Formally, the rate

61

of growth of f can be obtained directly from Definition 14.2.1. Clearly, n^2 is $O(f)$. Conversely,

$$
\begin{aligned}
n^2 + 5 \cdot n + 2 + 10/n \quad &\leq \quad n^2 + 5 \cdot n^2 + 2 \cdot n^2 + 10 \cdot n^2 \\
&= \quad 18 \cdot n^2
\end{aligned}
$$

for all $n > 0$. Thus $f = O(n^2)$. Combining the two relationships we see that f and n^2 have the same rates of growth.

4. d) To show that the factorial function provides an upper bound to the growth of the exponential function 2^n, we prove that $n! > 2^n$ for all $n \geq 4$.

$$
\begin{aligned}
n! \quad &= \quad \prod_{i=0}^{n} i \\
&= \quad 2 \cdot 3 \cdot 4 \cdot \prod_{i=5}^{n} i \\
&> \quad 2^4 \cdot \prod_{i=5}^{n} i \\
&> \quad 2^4 \cdot \prod_{i=5}^{n} 2 \\
&> \quad 2^n
\end{aligned}
$$

4. e) The inequality $n! > 2^n$ for $n \geq 4$, established in Exercise 4 d), is used to prove that $n! \neq O(2^n)$. Assume that $n! = O(2^n)$. Then there are constants c and n_0 such that

$$
n! \leq c \cdot 2^n.
$$

whenever $n \geq n_0$. Let m be a number greater than the maximum of n_0, $2 \cdot c$, and 4. Then

$$
\begin{aligned}
m! \quad &= \quad m \cdot (m-1)! \\
&> \quad 2 \cdot c \cdot (m-1)! \\
&> \quad 2 \cdot c \cdot 2^{m-1} \\
&= \quad c \cdot 2^m
\end{aligned}
$$

Consequently, there are no constants that satisfy the requirements of Definition 14.2.1 and $n! \neq O(2^n)$.

7. a) The Turing machine M reduces the problem of recognizing the language $L_1 = \{a^i b^i a^j \mid i, j \geq 0\}$ to that of recognizing $L_2 = \{c^i d^i \mid i \geq 0\}$.

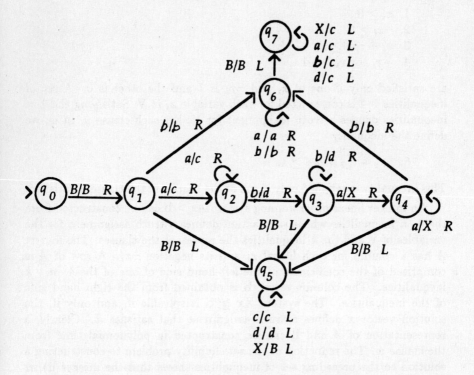

If the input string has the form $a^i b^k a^j$, the computation of M produces the string $c^i d^k$. This string will be accepted by a machine that recognizes L_2 only if $i = k$. Computations of M with any other input produces a string consisting solely of c's, which will be rejected by a machine that recognizes L_2.

15. To show that the integer linear programming is NP-hard, we reduce the question of the satisfiability of a 3-conjunctive normal form formula to that of satisfying a system of integral inequalities. Let

$$w = u_1 \wedge u_2 \wedge \cdots \wedge u_k$$

be a 3-conjunctive normal form formula with clauses $u_i = v_{i,1} \vee v_{i,2} \vee v_{i,3}$ and let $V = \{x_1, x_2, \ldots, x_n\}$ be the set of Boolean variables occuring in w.

We will consider the literals as variables that may assume integer values. For each pair of literals x_i and $\neg x_i$ in V, the four equations

1. $x_i \geq 0$
2. $\neg x_i \geq 0$
3. $x_i + \neg x_i \geq 1$
4. $-x_i - \neg x_i \geq -1$

are satisfied only if one of x_i and $\neg x_i$ is 1 and the other is 0. A set of inequalities 1–4 is constructed for each variable x_i in V. Satisfying the $4 \cdot n$ inequalities defines a truth assignment for V. For each clause u_i in w, we define the inequality

5. $v_{i,1} + v_{i,2} + v_{i,3} \geq 1$.

This inequality is satisfied only if one of the literals in the clause is satisfied.

An integer linear programming system $Ax \geq b$ can be constructed from the $4 \cdot n$ inequalities whose satisfaction defines a truth assignment for the variables of V and the k inequalities the represent the clauses. The matrix A has a column for each literal x_i and its negation $\neg x_i$. A row of A is comprised of the coefficients of the left-hand side of one of the $4 \cdot n + k$ inequalities. The column vector b is obtained from the right-hand side of the inequalities. The system $Ax \geq b$ is solvable if, and only if, the solution vector x defines a truth assignment that satisfies w. Clearly, a representation of A and b can be constructed in polynomial time from the clause w. The reduction of the satisfiability problem to constructing a solution to the preceding set of inequalities shows that the integer linear programming problem is NP-hard.

Chapter 15

LL(k) Grammars

1. **a)** The lookahead sets are given for the rules of the grammar. The lookahead set for a variable A is the union of the lookahead sets of the A rules.

rule	lookahead set
$S \to ABab$	$\{abab, acab, aab, cbab, ccab, cab\}$
$S \to bAcc$	$\{bacc, bccc\}$
$A \to a$	$\{abab, acab, aab, acc\}$
$A \to c$	$\{cbab, ccab, cab, ccc\}$
$B \to b$	$\{bab\}$
$B \to c$	$\{cab\}$
$B \to \lambda$	$\{ab\}$

2. b) The $FIRST_1$ and $FOLLOW_1$ sets for the variables of the grammar are

variable	$FIRST_1$	$FOLLOW_1$
S	$a, \#$	λ
A	a	$a, \#$
B	a	$\#$

To determine whether the grammar is LL(1), the techniques outlined in Theorem 15.2.5 are used to construct the lookahead sets from the $FIRST_1$ and $FOLLOW_1$ sets.

65

rule	lookahead set
$S \to AB\#$	$\{a, \#\}$
$A \to aAb$	$\{a\}$
$A \to B$	$\{a, \#\}$
$B \to aBc$	$\{a\}$
$B \to \lambda$	$\{\#\}$

Since the lookahead sets for the alternative A rules both contain the symbol a, the grammar is not strong LL(1).

3. a) Algorithm 15.4.1 is used to construct the $FIRST_2$ sets for each of the variables of the grammar. The rules of the grammar produce the following assignment statements for Step 3.2 of the algorithm.

$$F(S) := F(S) \cup trunc_2(F'(A)F'(B)F'(C)\{cc\})$$

$$F(A) := F(A) \cup trunc_2(\{a\}F'(A)) \cup \{a\}$$

$$F(B) := F(B) \cup trunc_2(\{b\}F'(B))$$

$$F(C) := F(C) \cup trunc_2(\{c\}F'(C)) \cup \{a, b, c\}$$

The algorithm is traced by exhibiting the sets produced after each iteration.

step	$F(S)$	$F(A)$	$F(B)$	$F(C)$
0	$\emptyset$	$\emptyset$	$\{\lambda\}$	$\emptyset$
1	$\emptyset$	$\{a\}$	$\{\lambda, b\}$	$\{a, b, c\}$
2	$\{aa, ab, ac\}$	$\{a, aa\}$	$\{\lambda, b, bb\}$	$\{a, b, c, ca, cb, cc\}$
3	$\{aa, ab, ac\}$	$\{a, aa\}$	$\{\lambda, b, bb\}$	$\{a, b, c, ca, cb, cc\}$

The rules that contain a variable on the right-hand side generate the assignment statements used in Steps 3.2.2 and 3.2.3 of Algorithm 15.5.1. The rules $S \to ABC\#\#, B \to bB$ and $C \to cC$ produce

$$FL(C) := FL(C) \cup trunc_2(\{\#\#\}FL'(S))$$
$$= FL(C) \cup \{\#\#\}$$

$$FL(B) := FL(B) \cup trunc_2(FIRST_2(C)\{\#\#\}FL'(S))$$
$$= FL(B) \cup \{a\#, b\#, c\#, ca, cb, cc\}$$

$$FL(A) := FL(A) \cup trunc_2(FIRST_2(B)FIRST_2(C)\{\#\#\}FL'(S))$$
$$= FL(A) \cup \{a\#, b\#, c\#, ba, bb, bc\}$$

$$FL(B) := FL(B) \cup FL'(B)$$

$$FL(C) := FL(C) \cup FL'(C)$$

The last two assignment statements may be omitted from consideration since they do not contribute to the generation of $FL(B)$ and $FL(C)$.

step	$FL(S)$	$FL(A)$	$FL(B)$	$FL(C)$
0	$\{\lambda\}$	$\emptyset$	$\emptyset$	$\emptyset$
1	$\{a\#, b\#, c\#, ba, bb, bc\}$	$\{a\#, b\#, c\#, ca, cb, cc\}$	$\{\#\#\}$	$\emptyset$
2	$\{a\#, b\#, c\#, ba, bb, bc\}$	$\{a\#, b\#, c\#, ca, cb, cc\}$	$\{\#\#\}$	$\emptyset$

The length two lookahead sets are used to construct the $FIRST_2$ and $FOLLOW_2$ sets.

rule	lookahead set
$S \rightarrow ABC\#\#$	$\{aa, ab, ac\}$
$A \rightarrow aA$	$\{aa\}$
$A \rightarrow a$	$\{aa, ab, ac\}$
$B \rightarrow bB$	$\{ba, bb, bc\}$
$B \rightarrow \lambda$	$\{a\#, b\#, c\#, ca, cb, cc\}$
$C \rightarrow cC$	$\{ca, cc, cc\}$
$C \rightarrow a$	$\{a\#\}$
$C \rightarrow b$	$\{b\#\}$
$C \rightarrow c$	$\{c\#\}$

The lookahead sets of the A rules show that the grammar is not strong LL(2).

4. We must show that the identity

$$FIRST_k(au) = \{av \mid v \in FIRST_{k-1}(u)\}$$

holds for all $k \geq 1$. For convenience we let $FIRST_0(u) = \{\lambda\}$ for all strings u. Let $v \in FIRST_{k-1}(u)$ for some $k \geq 1$. This implies that there is a derivation $u \overset{*}{\Rightarrow} vx$ where $vx \in \Sigma^*$, $length(v) = k - 1$ or $length(v) < k - 1$ and $x = \lambda$. Consequently, $au \overset{*}{\Rightarrow} avx$ and av is in $FIRST_k(au)$.

The preceding argument shows that $FIRST_k(au) \subseteq \{a\}FIRST_{k-1}(u)$. We must now establish the opposite inclusion. Let $av \in FIRST_{k-1}(au)$. Then $au \overset{*}{\Rightarrow} avx$ where $length(v) = k - 1$ or $length(v) < k - 1$ and $x = \lambda$. The derivation $u \overset{*}{\Rightarrow} vx$, obtained by deleting the a from the preceding derivation, shows that $v \in FIRST_{k-1}(u)$.

6. a) The lookahead sets for the rules of G_1 are

rule	lookahead set
$S \to aSb$	$\{a^j a^i c^i b^j \mid j > 0, i \geq 0\}$
$S \to A$	$\{a^i c^i \mid i \geq 0\}$
$A \to aAc$	$\{a^i c^i \mid i > 0\}$
$A \to \lambda$	$\{\lambda\}$

For any $k > 0$, the string a^k is a lookahead string for both of the S rules. Thus G_1 is not strong $LL(k)$.

A pushdown automaton that accepts $L(G_1)$ is defined by the following transitions.

$$\delta(q_0, a, \lambda) = [q_1, A]$$
$$\delta(q_1, a, \lambda) = [q_1, A]$$
$$\delta(q_1, b, A) = [q_2, \lambda]$$
$$\delta(q_1, c, A) = [q_3, \lambda]$$
$$\delta(q_2, b, A) = [q_2, \lambda]$$
$$\delta(q_3, b, A) = [q_2, \lambda]$$
$$\delta(q_3, c, A) = [q_3, \lambda]$$

States q_0 and q_1 read an a and push A onto the stack. State q_3 reads the c's and q_2 the b's with each transition popping the stack. The accepting states are q_0 and q_2.

8. a) The process of transforming the grammar into an equivalent strong $LL(1)$ grammar begins by removing the directly left recursive A rules.

$$S \to A\#$$
$$A \to aB \mid ZaB$$
$$B \to bBc \mid \lambda$$
$$Z \to bZ \mid cZ \mid b \mid c$$

The resulting grammar is not strong $LL(1)$ since there are two Z rules that begin with b and two that begin with c. Left factoring these rules we obtain

$$S \rightarrow A\#$$
$$A \rightarrow aB \mid ZaB$$
$$B \rightarrow bBc \mid \lambda$$
$$Z \rightarrow bX \mid cY$$
$$X \rightarrow Z \mid \lambda$$
$$Y \rightarrow Z \mid \lambda$$

Examining the length one lookahead sets, we see that this grammar is strong LL(1).

rule	lookahead set
$S \rightarrow A\#$	$\{a, b, c\}$
$A \rightarrow ab$	$\{a\}$
$A \rightarrow Zab$	$\{b, c\}$
$B \rightarrow bBc$	$\{b\}$
$B \rightarrow \lambda$	$\{\#\}$
$Z \rightarrow bX$	$\{b\}$
$Z \rightarrow cY$	$\{c\}$
$X \rightarrow Z$	$\{b, c\}$
$X \rightarrow \lambda$	$\{a\}$
$Y \rightarrow Z$	$\{b, c\}$
$Y \rightarrow \lambda$	$\{a\}$

10. The lookahead sets for the grammar G_1 are

rule	lookahead set
$S \rightarrow aAcaa$	$\{aacaa, aabcaa, acaa\}$
$S \rightarrow bAbcc$	$\{babcc, babbcc, bbcc\}$
$A \rightarrow a$	$\{acaa, abcc\}$
$A \rightarrow ab$	$\{abcaa, abbcc\}$
$A \rightarrow \lambda$	$\{caa, bcc\}$

One symbol lookahead is sufficient to discriminate between the S rules. Four symbols are required to choose the appropriate A rule. Thus G_1 is strong LL(4).

To show that G_1 is LL(3), the lookahead sets are constructed for the sentential forms of the grammar.

rule	sentential form	lookahead set
$S \rightarrow aAcaa$	S	$\{aaccaa, aabcaa, acaa\}$
$S \rightarrow bAbcc$	S	$\{babcc, babbcc, bbcc\}$
$A \rightarrow a$	$aAcaa$	$\{acaa\}$
$A \rightarrow ab$	$aAcaa$	$\{abcaa\}$
$A \rightarrow \lambda$	$aAcaa$	$\{caa\}$
$A \rightarrow a$	$bAbcc$	$\{abcc\}$
$A \rightarrow ab$	$bAbcc$	$\{abbcc\}$
$A \rightarrow \lambda$	$bAbcc$	$\{bcc\}$

Chapter 16

LR(k) Grammars

1. a) The LR(0) contexts for the rules of G_1 are obtained from the right-most derivations

$$S \Rightarrow AB \overset{i}{\Rightarrow} Ab^i B \Rightarrow Ab^i a \overset{j}{\Rightarrow} a^j Ab^i B \Rightarrow a^j bb^i a$$

rule	LR(0) contexts
$S \to AB$	$\{AB\}$
$A \to aA$	$\{a^i A \mid i > 0\}$
$A \to b$	$\{a^i b \mid i \geq 0\}$
$B \to bB$	$\{Ab^i B \mid i > 0\}$
$B \to a$	$\{Ab^i a \mid i \geq 0\}$

The nondeterministic LR(0) machine of G_1 is constructed directly from the specifications of Definition 16.3.2.

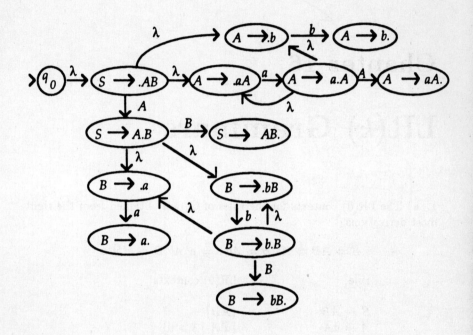

The deterministic LR(0) machine of G_1 is

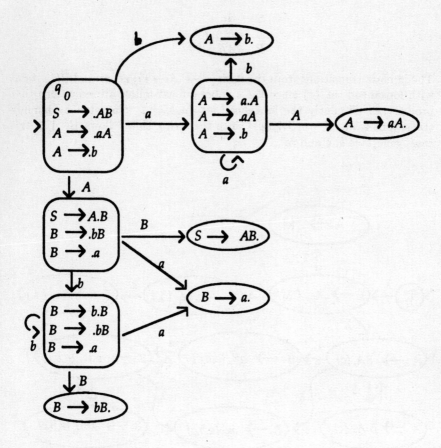

Since every state with a complete item contains only that item, the grammar G_1 is LR(0).

3. The grammar AE is not LR(0) since A is an LR(0) context of the rule $S \to A$ and a viable prefix of the rule $A \to A + T$.

7. a) The nondeterministic LR(1) machine is constructed for the grammar

$$S \rightarrow Ac$$
$$A \rightarrow BA \mid \lambda$$
$$B \rightarrow aB \mid b$$

The lambda transitions from the item $[S \rightarrow .Ac, \{\lambda\}]$ generate LR(1) items with lookahead set $\{c\}$ since the symbol c must follow all reductions that produce A. Similarly the lookahead set $\{a, b, c\}$ is generated by lambda transitions from $[A \rightarrow .BA, \{c\}]$ since the string that follows B, A in this case, generates b, c and λ.

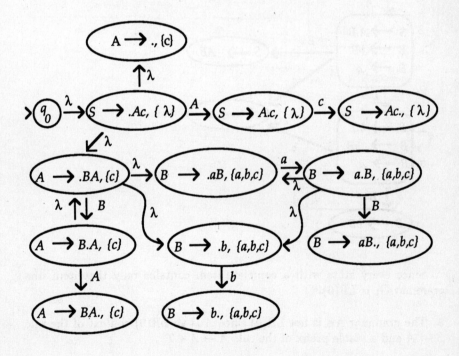

The corresponding deterministic LR(1) is

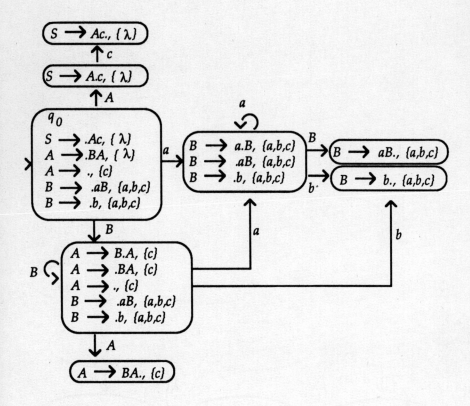

Since the deterministic machine satisfies the conditions of Definition 16.5.3, the grammar is LR(1).